WHAT OTHERS ARE SAYING ABOUT

WHITEWASHING THE FENCE

Keith Potter not only understands the challenge of leading leaders—he's mastered the task. And now he's organized and documented his methods for our benefit. With the perfect overlay of Tom Sawyer, enjoying the efforts of others while they immerse themselves in painting the fence, you will benefit from Keith's new insights into modern leadership.
Kevin Compton, Venture Capitalist

If you are going to read one leadership book today, Whitewashing the Fence should be it. Keith Potter honors the sound wisdom of the past and carries it forward by laying out a relevant and authentic leadership philosophy for our time. Keith is the real deal. For over a decade, I have personally observed Keith successfully apply this leadership approach on an organizational and personal level, making a significant impact on many lives along the way.
Chris Trapani, Founder and CEO,
Sereno Group

Keith's leadership principles and insights transfer remarkably well to the military arena. Whitewashing the Fence *should be on every military leader's professional reading list, especially 'leaders of leaders' in complex organizations. His practical lessons in servant-oriented, standards-based, results-driven leadership provide instant, lasting value to the leader striving for optimal organizational performance when failure is not an option.*

Mat Guerrieri, Lieutenant Colonel,
United States Army

As a business leader and football coach, I can say that every leader and coach can benefit from reading this book. A leader has to manage and massage "assistant coaches" in a way that's engaging and exciting so that they'll teach and champion the goals and values that lead to success. This book is a godsend to "head coaches" who want to get out ahead and prevent potentially harmful group dynamics.

Craig Awbrey, President,
Awbrey Development Co.

It takes leadership to inspire enthusiastic effort toward a common vision and a preferred future. Maximizing continual output from the vision's inspirational fuel pump remains a most challenging leadership mystery. Whitewashing the Fence *is a classic work that masterfully illustrates how to build a "high-authorization culture" and why it fuels maximum commitment and excellent performance by an inspired team. This is an essential toolkit for the 21st century leader!*

Bryan Hydzu, President,
Central California C12 Group, Inc.

2

Over decades of association with Keith Potter—teammate, classmate, boss and mentor--Keith is a true leader and a pleasure to work with! Learn from the extraordinary wisdom expressed in **Whitewashing the Fence.**

John W. Tastad, Program Coordinator
Advanced Care Planning, Sharp HealthCare

In **Whitewashing the Fence,** *Keith Potter has written a personal and cultural transformational leadership masterpiece! His High Authorization Leadership model will fuel leaders and their organizations to thrive at the highest levels.*

Steve Fedyski, President and CEO
Pinnacle Forum

Whitewashing the Fence

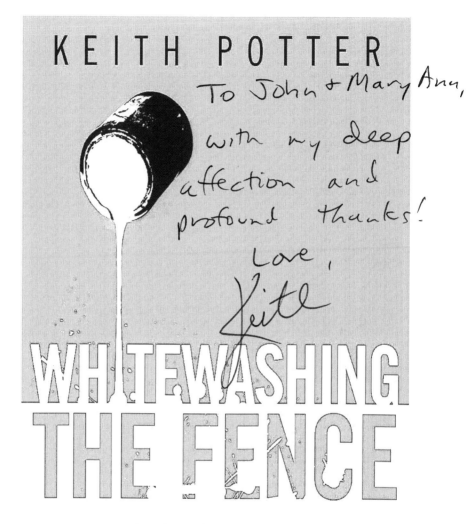

KEITH POTTER

WHITEWASHING THE FENCE

Leading Leaders in a Way That Works

To John & Mary Ann, with my deep affection and profound thanks! Love, Keith

Whitewashing the Fence: Leading Leaders in a Way that Works

Copyright © 2013[1] by Keith Potter

Published by Claywork Publishing, a division of ClayWork Productions, LLC, San Jose, California.

ISBN-13 978-0615721651
ISBN 0615721656

Scripture is taken from the HOLY BIBLE, NEW INTERNATIONAL VERSION®. NIV®. Copyright © 1973, 1978, 1984 by International Bible Society. Used by permission of Zondervan. All rights reserved.

Cover design: Jerry Lund.
Interior design: Jerry Lund
Interior photo: Kirsten Trapani

Printed in the United States of America

---

[1]

To

Paul E. Wright

**A tremendous leader in business,
and an even greater father-in-law.**

Whitewashing the Fence

CONTENTS

Section One: High Authorization Leadership

Section Two: A Culture Altering Strategy

Section Three: Some Practical Application

Whitewashing the Fence

Forward

Leadership is hard.

Leading leaders is even tougher. It will test the most confident and experienced of executives. Leading leaders in a largely volunteer setting, which is what Keith Potter has done, is a task for only the bravest among us.

Keith understands the challenge of leadership. He has mastered the task. And now he's organized and documented his methods for our benefit.

I've had the benefit of studying under Keith when he was the lead pastor of a large Silicon Valley church. He led parishioners in a church composed largely of high achieving women, men and families. Over the years, I marveled at the way he took on his calling, and I've been impressed by the way he empowered his staff. More personally, I watched him model fatherhood and a deep devotion to his wife.

Many times I took notes from Keith's messages with plans to use them the next day in my business life. More than once, I watched Keith handle complex circumstances in an even more complex organization in ways that challenged me to think about leadership in new ways.

I was so honored when Keith asked me to contribute to this book. I serve on the Board of Directors of numerous public and private technology companies and I serve as a partner in a high profile venture capital firm—both roles make me an avid observer of leadership. With that background, I jumped right into the book and found the style and content captivating. I only put the book down to send off quick notes or emails to other leaders in my network.

Make the investment. Read *Whitewashing the Fence* and you will know the answer to these leadership questions:

> *What do Tom Sawyer, Ronald Reagan, Bill Walsh, Mikhail Gorbachev, John Wooden and Jesus all share?*

> *How do you, as the person in charge, distribute authority without abdicating leadership?*

> *Where do you find enough grace to allow freedom, along with the gratitude to recognize results?*

Keith Potter reminds us that if Jesus could leave the greatest mission of all time to common people, we should be able to find leaders for our organizations.

But once we find these leaders, how do we manage and motivate them? Of course we want the best people, but how do we create a culture that helps them achieve the very best for the community they serve?

One more thing: it was enlightening to see how a thoughtful CEO sees a truly useful board. I've often wondered what a CEO really wants from a board. Direction? Insight? Accountability? Management? Just what do CEO's need in order to perform their duties and carry the organization forward?

For the first time in my career, I found a set of thoughtful parameters to create the right balance of all the needs for both the leader and the board member.

With the perfect overlay of Tom Sawyer, enjoying the efforts of others while they immerse themselves in painting the fence, you will benefit from Keith's new insights into modern leadership.

Kevin Compton, Co-Owner,
San Jose Sharks

Whitewashing the Fence

Preface

Tom Sawyer and the Fence

Tom appeared on the sidewalk with a bucket of whitewash and a long-handled brush. He surveyed the fence, and all gladness left him and deep melancholy settled down upon his spirit. Thirty yards of board fence nine feet high. Life to him seemed hollow, and existence but a burden. Sighing he dipped his brush and passed it along the topmost plank; repeated the operation; did it again; compared the insignificant whitewashed streak with the far-reaching continent of unwhitewashed fence, and sat down on a tree-box discouraged....

He began to think of the fun he had planned for this day, and his sorrows multiplied. Soon the free boys would come tripping along on all sorts of delicious expeditions, and they would make a world of fun of him *for having to work—the very thought of it burnt him like fire. He got out his worldly wealth and examined it—bits of toys, marbles and trash; enough to buy an exchange of work, maybe, but not half enough to buy so much as half an hour of pure freedom. So he returned his straitened means to his pocket, and gave up the idea of trying to buy the boys. At this dark and hopeless moment and inspiration burst upon him! Nothing less than a great, magnificent inspiration.*

He took up his brush and went tranquilly to work. Ben Rogers hove in sight presently—the very boy, of all boys, whose ridicule he had been dreading. Ben's gait was light and his anticipations high. He was eating an apple, and giving a long, melodious whoop, at intervals, followed by a deep-toned ding-dong-dong, ding-dong-dong, for he was personating a steamboat. As he drew near, he slackened speed, took the middle of the street, leaned far over the starboard and rounded to ponderously and with laborious pomp and circumstance—for he was personating the Big Missouri, and considered himself to be drawing nine feet of water. He was boat and captain and engine bells combined, so he had to imagine himself standing on his own hurricane deck giving the orders and executing them:

"Stop her, sir! Ting-a-ling-ling!" The headway ran almost out and he drew up slowly toward the sidewalk.

"Ship up to back! Ting-a-ling-ling!" His arms straightened and stiffened down his sides.

"Set her back on the stabboard! Ting-a-ling-ling! Chow! Ch-chow-wow! Chow!" His right hand, meantime, describing stately circles, for it was representing a forty-foot wheel.

"Stop the stabboard! Ting-a-ling-ling! Stop the labboard! Come ahead on the stabboard! Stop her! Let your outside turn over slow! Ting-a-ling-ling! Chow-ow-

ow! Get out that head-line! Lively now! Come—out with your spring-line-what're you about there! Take a turn round that stump with the bight of it! Stand by that stage, now—let her go! Done with the engines, sir! Ting-a-ling-ling! Sh't! s'h't! sh't!" (trying the gauge cocks).

Tom went on whitewashing—paid no attention to the steamboat. Ben stared a moment and then said:

"Hi-yi! You're up a stump, ain't you?"

No answer. Tom surveyed his last touch with the eye of an artist, then he gave his brush another gentle sweep and surveyed the result, as before. Ben ranged up along-side of him. Tom's mouth watered for the apple, but he stuck to his work. Ben said:

"Hello, old chap, you got to work, hey?"

Tom wheeled suddenly and said:

"Why, it's you, Ben! I warn't noticing."

"Say—I'm going in a-swimming, I am. Don't you wish you could? But of course you'd druther work—wouldn't you? Course you would!"

Tom contemplated the boy a bit, and said:

"What do you call work?"

"Why, ain't that work?"

Tom resumed his whitewashing, and answered carelessly: "Well, maybe it is, and maybe it ain't. All I know, is, it suits Tom Sawyer."

"Oh come, now, you don't mean to let on that you like it?"

The brush continued to move.

"Like it? Well, I don't see why I oughtn't to like it. Does a boy get a chance to whitewash a fence every day?"

That put the thing in a new light. Ben stopped nibbling his apple. Tom swept his brush daintily back and forth—stepped back to note the effect—added a touch here and there—criticized the effect again—Ben *watching every move and getting more and more interested, more and more absorbed. Presently he said:*

"Say, Tom, let me whitewash a little."

Tom considered, was about to consent; but he altered his mind:

"No—no—I reckon it wouldn't hardly do, Ben. You see, Aunt Polly's awful particular about this fence—right here on the street, you know—but if it was the back fence I wouldn't mind and she wouldn't. Yes, she's awful particular about this fence; it's got to be done very careful; I reckon there ain't one boy in a thousand, maybe two thousand, that can do it the way it's got to be done."

"No—is that so? Oh come, now—lemme just try. Only just a little—I'd let you, if you was me, Tom."

"Ben, I'd like to, honest injun; but Aunt Polly— well, Jim wanted to do it, but she wouldn't let him; Sid wanted to do it, and she wouldn't let Sid. Now don't you see how I'm fixed? If you was to tackle this fence and anything was to happen to it—."

"Oh, shucks, I'll be just as careful. Now lemme try. Say—I'll give you the core of my apple."

"Well, here—No, Ben, now don't. I'm afeard—"

"I'll give you all of it!"

Tom gave up the brush with reluctance in his face, but alacrity in his heart. And while the late steamer Big Missouri worked and sweated in the sun, the retired artist sat on a barrel in the shade close by, dangled his legs, munched his apple, and planned the slaughter of more innocents. There was no lack of material; boys happened along every little while; they come to jeer, but remained to whitewash. By the time Ben was fagged out, Tom had traded the next chance to Billy Fisher for a kite, in good repair; and when he played out, Johnny Miller bought in for a dead rat and a string to swing it with—and so on, and so on, hour after hour. And when the middle of the afternoon came, from being a poor poverty-stricken boy in the morning, Tom was literally rolling in wealth. He had besides the things before mentioned, twelve marbles, part of a jew's harp, a piece of blue bottle glass to look through, a spool cannon, a key that wouldn't unlock anything, a fragment of chalk, a glass stopper of a decanter, a tin soldier, a couple of tadpoles, six firecrackers, a kitten with only one eye, a brass doorknob, a dog collar—but no dog—the handle of a knife, four pieces of orange peel, and a dilapidated old window sash.

He had had a nice, good, idle time all the while— plenty of company—and the fence had three coats of whitewash on it! If he hadn't run out of whitewash, he would have bankrupted every boy in the village.

Tom said to himself that it was not such a hollow world, after all. He had discovered a great law of human action, without knowing it—namely, that in order to make a man or a boy covet a thing, it is only necessary to make the thing difficult to attain. If he had been a great and wise philosopher, like the writer of this book, he would now have comprehended that Work consists of whatever a body is obliged to do, and that Play consists of whatever a body is not obliged to do. And this would help him to understand why constructing artificial flowers or performing on a treadmill is work, while rolling tenpins or climbing Mont Blanc is only amusement. There are wealthy gentlemen in England who drive four-horse passenger coaches twenty or thirty miles on a daily line, in the summer, because the privilege costs them considerable money; but if they were offered wages for the service, that would turn it into work and then they would resign.

The boy mused a while over the substantial change which had taken place in his worldly *circumstances, and then wended toward headquarters to report.*[2]

---

[2] Excerpt from *The Adventures of Tom Sawyer* by Mark Twain.

Introduction

We were supposed to be sleeping. Instead, huddled under the covers with a flashlight, my brother Clark read to me Mark Twain's iconic tale of Tom Sawyer. Tom's keen imagination, adventurous spirit and magnetic ability to coax others into his exploits enraptured me.

The casual reader might accuse Tom Sawyer of trickery, laziness or both. In the opening episode of the book, Tom manipulates others to do his job—whitewashing the fence—so that he can goof off.

Still, Tom's adventure in delegation and authorization is more than one of the great moments in literature. It serves as a powerful model for leaders who, like Tom, want to see the work get done by others—and with pleasure.

Whitewashing the Fence is a life-changing journey into **high-authorization leadership**. For natural leaders who have an intuitive sense for breeding a culture of motivated achievers, *Whitewashing the Fence* will lend definition to behaviors that are instinctive and clarity to the task of reproducing leaders. For others, this study represents a huge paradigm shift that asks new questions and demands new models and behaviors. This shift may be painful and slow, but promises to be altogether rewarding. This entire book will help you empower others, grow your organization and enjoy yourself. It's not the only way to lead, but it's the best way.

Most of my views are born of observation and conviction. Some have been shaped or confirmed by good reading and thoughtful mentors. For twenty years, I've drawn on the partnership of enthusiastic teams of staff and volunteers to run, renew and launch non-profit organizations. As lead pastor of large churches, I served organizations with dozens of paid employees; but the real trick was inspiring and equipping thousands of church members to make the shift from consumer to fully enlisted coworker—and with pleasure.

The dynamics of leadership can be slightly different in volunteer organizations versus for-profit industry. Successful industry executives have said to me, "I could never do what you do. The church is the most complex leadership culture I can imagine. In industry, the bottom line is clear—profit. Employees are paid to perform and poor performers are fired. For the church and most non-profits, your bottom line is fuzzy and subject to so many opinions. And you can't fire volunteers. I'm not even sure you can fire paid employees without rocking the organization."

And they're right. Non-profits are complex organizations. As Jim Collins writes, "One corporate CEO turned academic dean tried to lead faculty toward his vision. The more he brought to bear his executive skill, the more the faculty decided they had better things to do than to attend the dean's faculty meetings. After all, what was he going to do? Fire them? They all had tenure."[3]

Collins suggests that **non-profit leadership "relies more upon persuasion, political currency and shared interests** to create the conditions for the right decision to happen." All of that is tough to rally and harness without executive authority undergirded by the power to withhold paychecks or dis-employ.

But **for-profit organizations aren't easy either,** especially in days when profits are harder to get hold of and top-heavy, authoritarian models are out of fashion. The task is the same—**trying to create a leadership culture that attracts, empowers and sustains the very best leaders**. You want a workplace where highly engaged leaders enlist, equip and inspire workers, and especially other leaders, to perform at high levels—and actually enjoy it. Even if positional authority exists with the power to demote or fire, **the best work will be done by people who want to be there**—people who are thrilled to be part of something big, functional and worthwhile.

That, ultimately, is my defense of Tom Sawyer. **His friends did not feel ill-used.** They aren't forced into service. In fact, they have fun. It's probably one of the best, most remarkable days of their idyllic Missouri childhoods—fictional days, of course.

It's not fiction to say that people need to find intense satisfaction in their work, or else they will walk away or give less than their best. **Realize that even paid**

---

[3] Collins, Jim. *Good to Great and the Social Sectors.* New York: HarperCollins, 2005.

employees are volunteers. No one is forcing them to show up and they can't be coerced into bringing their best energy and focus. The key is in **the art of *Whitewashing the Fence*.** We want everyone to *want* to show up and to bring a top-of-the-line effort.

This book will inspire you with lessons from great leaders in business, politics and sports. We'll even visit the life of the most influential person in history. Read, keep your mind open and put these things into practice.

Some say, "Practice makes perfect." One of my mentors used to say, "Perfect practice makes perfect." In other words, practicing the wrong thing isn't useful at all. And good practices, repeated over and over, lead to good things. In this case, perfect practice means intentionally unleashing imperfect leaders to make a huge impact on the working culture that you all lead together.

Some of you are tired. You've tried so hard and suffered a lot. Or you might feel like a failure, hungry for new models and tactics for inspiring the best in others. Or you might need renewal—a wind of fresh ideas to give you a reason to get out of bed and fight the battle.

This book will blow that fresh wind into your sails—even into your soul.

Section One

High Authorization
Leadership

Whitewashing the Fence

Chapter One

The Glorious Whitewasher

Not everything about **Tom Sawyer** is to be emulated. Tom is lazy, conniving and insincere. His motive for manipulating his friends has far more to do with his distaste for hard work, and less to do with great leadership. Moved by a better set of impulses, Tom might have mobilized his friends to paint the back fence, as well as the front, or he might have distributed his new-found wealth among all of his friends. He certainly wouldn't have tricked them into doing everything while he did nothing.

On the other hand, Tom did *anything but nothing.* **He was very busy doing what leaders do—enlisting, equipping, motivating and overseeing.** Under Tom's leadership, the fence received *three* coats of whitewash and his friends enjoyed hours of focus, productivity and experience in a task they would have to repeat later in life. Whatever the motive, Tom did a *service* for his Aunt Polly and for his friends.

Leadership is a form of service. It's a role most people are reluctant to play. It's a part many are not outfitted to play. It involves high risk and vulnerability, often neutralizing the rewards. Leadership is critical and costly and exciting and exhausting. Giving good leadership is giving a gift that benefits others.

As for Tom, he's moved by nobler motives later in the book. Nowhere, however, is he driven by keener instincts than in this first episode at Aunt Polly's fence. This is what happened.

Tom's Dreams are Bigger Than the Fence

Tom Sawyer is an adventurer. He dreams of faraway lands and great discoveries. With a paintbrush in hand, he ponders:

> *Cardiff Hill, beyond the village and above it... green with vegetation; and it lay just far enough away to seem a delectable land, dreamy, reposeful and exciting.*

Not everyone is built like Tom Sawyer. For dreamers like Tom, whitewashing a fence is painful labor. Climbing Cardiff Hill might require far more actual energy and exertion, but for people like Tom, climbing hills is invigorating. Painting fences isn't. When Tom first looked at the fence, "life to him seemed hollow and existence but a burden."

The Task Begs for More Hands

> *He dipped his brush and passed it along the topmost plank; repeated the operation; did it again; compared the insignificant whitewashed streak with the far-reaching continent of unwhitewashed fence, and sat down on a firebox discouraged.*

The job is simply too daunting for Tom alone and requires the help of others.

This is where would-be leaders fail to become leaders at all. Stubborn pride refuses to accept that other hands could do the task more quickly, more expertly and even more joyfully. **Actual laziness, fear of rejection, or an over-inflated perception of our own prowess trick us into doing ourselves what others could do better.** And we actually deny others the pleasure of partnership and usefulness because we choose to do the thing ourselves.

For example, I worked with an administrative assistant who has highly developed managerial skills. While I'd be okay if she only facilitated my needs and answered my requests—and nothing more—*she'll only be okay* if she's given the trust and freedom to create and oversee significant projects and events.

One season, she poured hours and energy into a vision-casting dinner, offering expertise and follow-through that I would have hurt myself and others trying to produce alone. At one point, she felt the strain of leading. I stupidly suggested that next year we should recruit a different project manager so that she wouldn't have to suffer the weight of it all. She nearly jumped out of her chair. "But this is what I do! This is what makes me feel like more than just a secretary! And this pain will pass. I *like* this!"

Lesson learned. I'd never devalued "just a secretary." But from my associate, I realized that most folks enjoy a greater share in the larger work.

It's like the old story of the two masons. The first seems tired and forlorn to a passerby, who asks, "What are you doing?"

"I'm stacking bricks."

The second mason appears energized and inspired. "What are *you* doing?" asks the observer.

"I'm building a cathedral to the glory of God!"

So part of *Whitewashing the Fence* is about sharing

actual responsibility for something big. Even more, it's about imparting perspective and inspiring a fresh spirit.

I want people around me who want to be full partners with a lively vision of what we're accomplishing.

Tom Knows Where to Find Partners for His Venture

> *He remembered that there was company at the pump . . . always waiting their turns, resting, trading playthings, quarreling, fighting, skylarking.*

One by one, they walk by. One after the other, Tom enlists them.

I keep lists in my files, on my desk and in my head. They are the *next people* to enlist. They are tomorrow's leaders. They are potential *hires*. Usually I stay in touch with these people, sometimes even building friendships so that future partnerships can be undergirded by mutual fondness and respect.

And I befriend people who live "at the pump," so they can help me identify and enlist the best people, and I can return the favor. One of my closest friends is a consultant who helps non-profits all over the country with their hiring. I do not befriend him so I can use his services. Our friendship is natural because we're in the same business—enlisting and mobilizing people to serve great purposes. Sometimes we meet for entire days at a time, simply to swap stories, insights, names and resources, and we never run out of conversation.

In his book, *Good to Great,* Jim Collins writes about "getting the right people on the bus" and "getting the right people in the right seats."[4] He considers this to be the biggest predictor of sustainable success. I agree. Few things debilitate any team like players who can't—or won't—

---

[4] Collins, Jim. *Good to Great.* New York: HarperCollins, 2001.

cooperate and contribute.

Of course, no one is perfect. Everyone brings deficits. The first key is to recruit and hire for character, and then teach ability. People who are unreliable or arrogant gum up the works in every conceivable way. While specific skills always matter—quite a lot in some roles—**I hire for character and train for skill.** I need people who are open to growth, eager to learn and not resistant to change.

The second key is to **place people in the correct roles.** I once hired an associate with extraordinary people skills and less-than-extraordinary management skills. I fashioned his role around his giftedness, and he succeeded. When I moved to another place, I was curious what my successor would do with this associate. Sadly, he piled programs onto his desk to be managed. Predictably, my friend lasted about one year. Then came the pain and residue of parting badly. My friend recovered—he's a champion—but in another field.

In another case, I inherited an associate who experienced moderate success working in one area, but was languishing because he isn't built for *moderate* success— he's also a champion. So we revisited his core gifts and training, refashioned his role and watched him succeed. Eventually he succeeded even more by accepting *my role* with another institution. He's absolutely "in the right seat on the bus."

A third key goes beyond Collins' admonitions about the "the bus." **When I hire people, I always fashion or refashion the job to fit that person.** I want to hire people who know who they are and have a pretty good notion for how to get the job done. If I hand someone an old job description and ask that person to do the job exactly the way a predecessor did it, then I must not have aspirations to see the organization go forward. Or else I have no confidence in the new person…which leads me to ask, "Why did I make this hire?"

At one position, I was handed a long and detailed job description. With respect for the intentions in which it was given, I cast off that job description as quickly as possible and wrote, with the counsel of supervisors, one that suited me. In truth, I felt humored by the notion that others were compelled to tell me how to do my job. I assumed they were hiring me for my competence and my own instincts for honoring core values and answering primary needs. And after all, the reason they hired me was to fix a system that they believed was broken.

That experience taught me to remember how it feels to have a heavy load of "how" dumped on a new associate. I want those I enlist to be completely authentic to who they are, and completely invested in the grand work we're doing together. If they can't bring value to the "how" independent from my constricted views of how to get it done, then I've surely hired the wrong people.

Tom Realizes That Money Isn't Enough of a Motivator

He got out his worldly wealth and examined it—bits of toys, marbles, and trash; enough to buy an exchange of work, maybe, but not half enough to buy so much as half an hour of pure freedom. So he returned his straitened means to his pocket and gave up the idea of trying to buy the boys.

Money is part of the equation, but it isn't enough. In a volunteer organization, this is obvious. Even in a for-profit enterprise, money isn't really enough. Sure, money helps, especially if the money is symbolic, representing an honest sense of value and appreciation. But other things matter more if we want the *best* efforts and energies from those we lead. And other motivators *really* matter more if we want their *sustained* interest and loyalty. **People need**

purpose. People want pleasure. Folks like to be part of a winning team. And everyone needs to be appreciated; especially bright, talented people, who could easily take their extraordinary skills elsewhere.

Tom Calls It Something Other Than Work

Sure, for Tom it would be pure work without the help and company of others. But Tom is able to *"put the thing in a new light."* Mark Twain comments at the end of the chapter:

> *Work consists of whatever a body is obliged [obligated] to do and . . . play consists of whatever a body is not obliged [obligated] to do . . . . There are wealthy gentlemen in England who drive four-horse passenger coaches twenty or thirty miles on a daily line in the summer, because the privilege costs them considerable money; but if they were offered wages for the service, that would turn it into work and then they would resign.*

Enlisting people is not about buying, but selling—**selling the notion of a grand, worthy venture that begs for their investment of time, talent and energy.** Anything less will bore the kind of person who flourishes in a high-authorization culture.

Why would it be boring to work merely for the big bucks or the great perks? Because those benefits come at the end of the day or the end of the month. **I'm interested in what people do in the heart of the day.** If we believe in what we're doing, we'll dive in and live with passion. If we're actually serving humanity by developing and offering a quality product or a useful service, and in a context of community, we have a worthy ethic, fully owned, that fuels our passions. I just don't believe a paycheck, no matter how large, has the force to pull us through the day with any real heart. Let the paycheck be the icing on the cake. I want to work with people who know *the cake* is to *do good* and *help people* with the best products and services and, therefore, with their best energies and talents.

I want people who want to be there. And I want people who want excellence, defined in terms that are clear and shared.

Tom Sets a High Standard

> *You see, Aunt Polly's awful particular about this fence – right here on the street, you know . . . . Yes, she's awful particular about this fence; it's got to be done very careful; I reckon there ain't one boy in a thousand, maybe two thousand that can do it the way it's got to be done.*

Of course, Tom is manipulating. Still, he's setting a standard for performance that's likely to make Aunt Polly happy and, at the same time, make others far more intrigued by the task. Any old job can hold us for a day, but a job that requires our best efforts will become more than a job—even an obsession.

Of course, obsessions can be bad. I'm not an advocate of hardcore workaholism, especially at the expense of family, community and overall health and balance.

But there are healthy obsessions. Itching to create, produce and serve is a good thing. If I don't hunger to show up for the hard work of the day ahead of me, then it might be time to talk to a career counselor; and if that doesn't work, perhaps another kind of counselor. But as a whole, I want to actually *want* to be there. And I hope to **be surrounded by others who want to be there.**

My best teachers and coaches were my most demanding ones. They set the bar high and then convinced me that the goals were worth my best energy and effort.

The teachers and coaches who set the bar low got little out of me—little effort, energy or even respect.

Twain notes that Tom:

> *had discovered a great law of human action, without knowing it—namely, that in order to make a man or a boy covet a thing, it is only necessary to make the thing difficult to attain.*

They Pay Tom for the Privilege

Again, we see the conniving side of Tom Sawyer. Without a spot of guilt, he receives pay from his friends for the privilege of doing this hard work on the fence. This wasn't his best moment.

Hopefully, we aren't users or abusers when it comes to compensating team members. Under the influence of God and conscience, we should be rattled by the growing disparity between executive pay and salaries down the line. That disparity proves our capacity for manipulation and greed.

But the disparity also proves how generously good leadership can be rewarded in this world and **how desperate organizations are to find and keep leaders who can mobilize and motivate others.**

To keep greed at bay, I like to remind myself, "I'm not being paid to do this job. I'm being paid so that I can fully apply myself." Especially in a non-profit setting, it helps to leave the matter of appropriate compensation to others and to reserve any posturing or negotiating for those moments that truly require it.

Even in the for-profit world, there are studies that show that the most sustained success stories include a chief executive who chooses to invest in others while receiving lower than average executive pay.

Still, leadership pays. It also costs, and sometimes dearly. But it pays.

Tom Enjoys the Companionship

Ultimately, Tom Sawyer is a social animal. One by-product of his whitewashing scheme is the fellowship. *He had a nice, good, and idle time all the while—plenty of fellowship....*

Not all strong leaders are social beasts, but for those who are, enlisting others is a welcome excuse to make friends and enlarge our notion of family.

I don't believe that creating a party atmosphere is the best way to make work a pleasure. As Dennis Bakke writes in *Joy at Work,* the greater source of pleasure is respect and shared responsibility. "The key to joy at work is the personal freedom to take actions and make decisions using individual skills and talents."[5]

But **there's a lot to be said for friendly interest, familial care and the fatherly (or sisterly or brotherly) touch.** Ordinary scrapes that cause abrasions in the workplace will simply not be as deep or lasting if relationships are genuine. Regular rhythms that necessitate seasons of a *full-court press* will seem more endurable if leaders prove their long-term interest in those who are pressing so hard.

And it's so much easier to *show* interest if we actually *are* interested. Every business is a people business, and if I don't actually *like* people or care about people, I might want to moderate that lack of concern by putting myself in a position of lesser influence.

That, of course, sounds ridiculous to some people who care *only* about product and profit. I assume that most

---

[5] Bakke, Dennis. *Joy at Work: A Revolutionary Approach to fun on the Job.* Seattle: PVG, 2006.

of them will struggle with the greater part of this book and might have lost interest already. God bless them—and God help us! The world, frankly, suffers that kind of leadership far too much.

It is possible to be relational, caring *and* productive. I suggest that this is the better way. After all, in Tom's care…

The Fence Gets Three Coats of Paint

The outcome is far greater than anything Tom could have manufactured without others. This is almost always true.

Not, perhaps, in the case of a work of art, or some exact project that requires the focused effort of a particular artisan.

But most leaders aren't artisans. If anything, leaders are much less genius than those who work for them. **The genius of leadership is finding prodigious talents and keeping them engaged.**

A wise and successful business leader in aerospace technology once told me, "I'm not the best engineer or the best money guy; but I find the best engineers and money people and I take care of them."

An equally successful executive in sports management told me the same thing. "I'm not the smartest about sports or money or business. But I find people smarter than me and figure out how to serve them well."

Whitewashing the Fence

Chapter Two

Two Fine Men

The 1980 presidential election presented me with my first opportunity to vote. Without any real political knowledge or savvy, I grabbed for familiar handles to guide my voting. My dad was more Republican and Mom more Democrat, though both claimed independence. Ronald Reagan was a popular figure. I'd seen him in black and white Westerns since I was a kid. But he was also an actor. Could we trust him?

     Jimmy Carter was earnest, fatherly and overtly committed to faith and a set of ethics that I shared. So I voted for Carter. He seemed so credible and obviously *good*. Even though his first term had been disastrous on various fronts, I thought the key was to have a good man bringing his influence to bear on the sticky world of politics, especially after the Richard Nixon debacle.

I was right in principle. Jimmy Carter might have been the finest *person* ever to sit in the Oval Office. He is certainly a generous and compassionate former president. His commitment to oppressed and impoverished people has only accented what most of us knew from the beginning—this man practices what he preaches. Jimmy Carter has the best interest of everyday people in mind. This is an authentic man.

But I learned, as the years passed, how misguided my vote was.

A Portrait of a Leader

First, I learned that **Ronald Reagan was also a good man.** Even his own children, who didn't always agree with his political views, vouch for his character, faith, kindness and general good will. Those who decry "cold conservatism" have a hard time making that label stick on such a genuinely warm man.

Second, I learned about leadership. Ronald Reagan was **a masterful leader.** He moved a nation out of a stifling pessimism and into a long season of optimism. He virtually won the Cold War and rescued the world (with another hero of mine, Mikhail Gorbachev) from the curse of eminent nuclear holocaust. He held stubbornly to a set of ideals and behaviors that he believed would bring the downfall of communism. And he stoked our economy into a season of unprecedented prosperity.

History already paints Reagan in fairly glowing terms. Since most histories and media commentaries are tilted to the left, right-leaning Reagan was even more effective than posterity is likely to admit.

No Slight Intended to a Great Person

To Jimmy Carter's credit, his low "quarterback

ratings" were due, in part, to the circumstances of the day. The Iran hostage crisis and numerous economic woes were not really of his making. And Richard Nixon's dishonesty followed by Gerald Ford's pardon of Nixon left the Oval Office riddled with intrigue and distrust. And, frankly, no one can get to the White House without exhibiting great leadership, and Carter did accomplish that.

Still, the common view of Carter's presidency goes something like this:

> Carter's presidency is rated as one of the ten worst in U.S. history, and he is often described as an ineffective and miserable president, who alienated many Washington insiders and members of Congress. On the other hand, it can be said that Carter gave the country an administration that was marked by integrity and high-mindedness, despite severe constraints.[6]

Those who describe Carter's "ineffective" leadership tend to talk about **micromanagement**. Carter was a brilliant man, an avid learner and an engineer. He was *into* details. He wedged himself into numerous functional circles of influence and wore himself out, along with others, by imposing himself everywhere. My lasting memory of Carter's presidency is the astonishing rate at which he aged during those four years. He looked so tired, and so did the country.

Another Way

Reagan, on the other hand, **infuriated his critics by looking fresh and optimistic** during the worst of crises. Comedians joked about his naps, vacations and overall

---

[6] Smith, Carter. *Presidents: All You Need to Know.* Irvington: Hylas Publishing, 2005.

jolliness. His inattention to detail opened the door for cartoonists to lampoon him as stupid and out of touch. Yet as our oldest president, he also seemed like one of the healthiest. Forever a cowboy, Reagan's friendly swagger fairly symbolized the spirit of America in a day when the Soviet Union was losing heart and giving way.

Among the many descriptions of Reagan's leadership, most sound like this:

> A new style of leadership that downplayed his role as administrator and emphasized the use of news media to communicate with the public.[7]

Those are the hallmarks of his leadership style. First, Reagan **authorized and entrusted others** to play significant roles in policy and practice. Second, he **used the emerging media culture** to teach, preach, persuade, reassure and altogether immerse the nation in his brand of entrepreneurial optimism and personal responsibility.

While Reagan was idealistic in his appeals, he was ultimately pragmatic in his leadership philosophy.

> It is not my intention to do away with government. It is rather to make it work – work with us, not over us; stand by our side, not ride on our back. Government can and must provide opportunity, not smother it; foster productivity, not stifle it.[8]

High Trust, High Authorization

In short, Reagan believed in people. Highly **trusting by nature**, he dared to forge a real relationship

---

[7] Ibid.
[8] Ibid.

with the president of an evil empire (U.S.S.R.). **Hopeful by nature**, he dared to believe that a new generation of my peers would take responsibility for the future of American government, business and civic life.

Our response? We literally cut our hair, put our ties back on and went to work. Yes, we were still plagued by drugs, sexual wantonness and boomer materialism, but we dared to believe with him—or else we benefited from Reagan while routinely mocking him (mine can be a generation of hypocrites).

It's true that Reagan's loose administrative style **left the door open for scandal**. In a complex world like politics, a trusting leader is subject to every abuse of freedom among staff and associates. Reagan's tenure was plagued by such scandals. Still, somehow, Reagan was fairly unmarked and his agenda unhindered in a greater current of productivity. He believed in people and people stepped up.

> We who live in free market societies believe that growth, prosperity and ultimately human fulfillment, are created from the bottom up, not the government down. Only when the human spirit is allowed to invent and create, only when human beings are given a personal stake in deciding economic policies . . . only then can societies remain economically alive, dynamic, progressive and free.[9]

History Proves It

Reagan was right. And I was right to vote for Reagan for a second term in 1984. While I'll always respect Jimmy Carter as a person, the leader I'll more likely

---

[9] Ibid.

emulate is Reagan. I will authorize and entrust other leaders around me.

The tired phrase, "If you want something done well, do it yourself," is a lie in the realm of leadership. I've tried it, and I've hurt myself with stress and hurt others with disrespect. **I've been the bottleneck of organizations** and my own worst enemy whenever I've backslidden into heavy, detailed management behaviors. And I've seen others do the same and worse. I refuse *not* to trust people and instead am determined to empower them!

I'll use every vehicle available to **communicate driving values and raging optimism.** Some organizations allow leaders to give strong, directive leadership by simply issuing orders with the incentive of money and the fear of dismissal. But the best leadership is persuasive leadership. As Jim Collins writes, **"True leadership only exists if people follow when they have the freedom not to."[10]**

That persuasion is usually born out of effective communication using every means available. And if the chief isn't a great communicator, the smart leader's first step is to enlist one.

And then I'll trust the creativity and determination of the people to create groundswells and upsurges of entrepreneurial invention. The most invasive and sustained programs in the organizations that I've served have been born out of the ideas and passions of others—not me—and my greater service to the organization was more about clearing the runway for innovators to take off, or creating a launching pad for creative people to fire off rockets to the moon.

Sociologist Lyle Schaller describes two kinds of change agents: those who create and innovate and those

---

[10] Collins, Jim. *Good to Great and the Social Sectors.* New York: HarperCollins, 2005.

who run interference for them, instigating a culture that is warm to new approaches.[11] I am the latter kind.

Yes, **we have successful models of strong, controlling leaders** who believe that "my way is the best way—the only way." Steve Jobs drove Apple to the top with overt, shameless megalomania. While my opinion is based only on his biography and my own years in the Silicon Valley, it looks to me like he could have gone higher, faster, farther if he had figured out a way to enlist and empower others more effectively. His bursts of micromanagement and scare tactics certainly set the bar for excellence very high; but there are other ways to inspire brilliance without creating a legacy of being known as "a jerk" or worse.

Reagan got called a jerk, mostly by people who abhorred his political platform, or snarked at him for a memory lapse, or for his afternoon naps.

But his strategies worked wonders, even while he was adored by people working in his periphery. Ronald Reagan was a smart man.

So I'll take naps and vacations and allow myself to be criticized for my inattention to detail. **People don't have to understand me in order to benefit from my approach**. And a little teasing brings us all together, knocks me down a rung or two and gives everyone the chance to **honor the detail-people** around me who glue together much of what we do.

I believe in giving people freedom to really lead and innovate. No, I don't want to leave room for scandal and the abuse of freedom. So I'll teach accountability and invest in relationships that guard against abuse. I'm also learning to set up other safeguards, like clear position descriptions, reasonable goals, honest evaluations,

---

[11] Schaller, Lyle. *The Change Agent: The Strategy of Innovative Leadership*. Abingdon Press, 1972.

meaningful staff meetings and staff retreats. **The best accountability happens in relationship.**

But I won't stunt freedom or burden emerging leaders with heavy, top-down governance. **Every organization, like good government, should "work with people, not over them;** stand by people, not ride on their backs." We can and must provide opportunity, not smother it; foster productivity, not stifle it. Our cause is to serve well and our commodity is hope. I want us to enjoy a culture that is "alive, dynamic, progressive and free."

Reagan didn't lead this way so that he could take a nap under a tree and kick back like Tom Sawyer. He believed in what he was doing and why. And I believe in this approach.

The demographics of my working world only amplify the need for this model. While serving and coaching leaders and world-changers, I need models that respect their autonomy, self-initiation and personal passion for changing the world. I want to be a catalyst and a coach, not a controller or a curmudgeon. I believe in people—their dreams, their gifts, their potentials. The Bible talks about a day when the *young will dream dreams and the old will have visions; women and men will speak the mind of God.*[12] I want that day to be now.

Sometimes, that means getting out of the way and trusting the power and voice of God in the lives of others—and coming alongside *their* visions instead of forcing them to cooperate with mine.

Whatever your field, get out of the way. Entrust key people with the authority and confidence to take your entire enterprise to heights and goals that you cannot achieve without them.

---

[12] *Acts* 2:17

Chapter Three

About Playing Quarterback

Serving as a leader in any organization is a lot like playing quarterback on a football team. A quarterback calls the team into a huddle, where he inspires his teammates and calls the plays. The quarterback receives and delivers the ball, often after adjusting to the defense and calling out audibles—on-the-spot adaptations to the offensive strategy. The quarterback influences pace of play and interacts with the referees. He's the coach on the field.

The quarterback is also the most vulnerable player, since most of the hits received by the quarterback are delivered in a moment that leaves him virtually defenseless, unable to lower a shoulder or dodge a blow. Yet much of the burden for a team's success is laid squarely on his shoulder pads. He knows this. His teammates know this. The coach, the spectators and the journalists know this.

In almost any organization, **someone plays quarterback**—calling out signals, inspiring, correcting, strategizing and delivering the ball—and taking some hits, too. It's a huge rush to play this position, and a huge responsibility.

Obviously, some quarterbacks are more successful than others. As I first wrote these words, the National Football League's leading quarterback by yards and touchdowns (Peyton Manning) squared off against Tom Brady, who has a penchant for winning Super Bowls (three). In truth, each quarterback battles the defense of the opposing team, and not each other. But in the eyes of a watching world, they're vying with each other. So two superstars in a colossal sport were matching wits and skills.

Manning was coming off the most prolific season in NFL history. He passed Dan Marino's Ruthian record for touchdown passes in a season. In the closing moments of the last regular season game of the year, Manning won the game and broke the record with flair. He's a fine quarterback and a sure Hall-of-Famer.

Brady, unlike Manning, owns few regular season records. He just wins Super Bowls. The week I wrote this chapter, as predicted, Brady's Patriots beat Manning's Colts handily.

The Truth About Quarterbacks

Quarterbacks don't play alone. All players and coaches affect outcomes. Still, there's something familiar and predictable about the outcome just mentioned. In NFL Super Bowl history, **most winners have not been statistical record-breakers.** Bart Starr of the Green Bay Packers won two Super Bowls and three championships in the years before there was a Super Bowl. Bob Griese of the

Miami Dolphins won two consecutive Super Bowls. The Dallas Cowboys' Roger Staubach also won two Super Bowls. Troy Aikman, from the same team, claimed three championships. Tom Brady has three under his belt. Joe Montana, a San Francisco 49er, claimed four titles.[13] All of these legendary figures had much in common. They didn't have the strongest arms in the league. They usually didn't have the biggest statistical numbers, though a few won passing titles in championship years (Starr, Staubach and Montana, once each). Yet these *are* the guys with multiple rings.

Always Some Exceptions . . . Still

Terry Bradshaw won four Super Bowls with the Steelers, and Bradshaw probably *did* have the strongest arm. John Elway of the Broncos won two Super Bowls with, perhaps, the strongest arm and best overall skills in NFL history.

However, Bradshaw had a supporting cast loaded with future hall-of-famers. And Elway didn't win Super Bowls until his last years when his physical prowess was diminishing while his overall capacity to win was emerging. When Elway won Super Bowls, he won with a balanced attack, a strong supporting cast and a notable change in approach—he *quit trying to do too much.*

The Curse of Talent

Talent can be a curse. Brett Favre of Green Bay Packer fame was tough and talented. He won one Super Bowl. Still, he'll always be known as the quarterback who too often tried to do too much.

---

[13] Sports Illustrated (Editor). *Sports Illustrated: Almanac 2005.* Sports Illustrated, 2005.

Steve Young of the San Francisco 49ers also won once, but should have ducked a few more collisions and avoided a few more concussions. He tried to do too much.

Fran Tarkenton of the Minnesota Vikings, the greatest scrambler in NFL history, once held numerous all-time records, but never won the big one.

Dan Marino of the Miami Dolphins, who broke most of Tarkenton's records and holds them still, suffered the same curse.

Michael Vick, one of today's superstars, is an enormous talent. But he's likely to suffer a similar fate.

Quarterbacks who can *do it all* rarely get what they ultimately want—Super Bowl victories.

Move the Ball Around

Why? Living for years in the Bay Area, I've always admired Joe Montana. He's a great sports hero and a prime example of *"Whitewashing"* principles. For one thing, he had a Tom Sawyer-like impishness—a love for the game.

But there's more. In Roger Craig's book, *Tales from the San Francisco 49ers Sideline,* the 49er's star tailback describes Montana like this:

> Joe Montana was not the most physically gifted quarterback, but he was smarter than any quarterback who ever stepped onto the field. Joe knew how to get rid of that ball on time and get it into the hands of guys who could make plays.[14]

And that's the key—getting rid of the ball on time and getting it into the hands of people who can make plays.

---

[14] Craig, Roger; Bill Walsh, and Matt Maiocco. *Tales from the San Francisco 49ers Sideline.* Champaign: Sports Publishing LLC, 2004.

The greatest quarterbacks, like the best leaders, **know how to move the ball around, include others and trust teammates to deliver.** Those who try to do too much by themselves ultimately under-perform.

Just as football is the ultimate team sport, other organizations require significant contributions from a host of role-players. The best organizational quarterbacks empower players with real responsibility and trust that teammates will step up and perform.

The Problem with "Happy Feet"

Craig also says of Montana:

> In the ultimate team spirit, I could not have been happier to have Joe Montana as my quarterback . . . . He stuck to the system because he knew the system worked . . . he could also improvise.... But what made our offense work so well for so long is that he went through his progression of receivers without any hint of panic or urgency.[15]

Poise in the pocket is a football phrase meaning, "Stand up tall, trust blockers to provide a pocket of protection, let receivers get to the open places in the field and deliver the ball." Great quarterbacks have poise in the pocket.

The ultra-talented tend to get *happy feet.* Instead of standing tall and trusting others, the temptation is to dance around, abandon the pocket of protection provided by the blockers and resort to dramatic improvisations that often impress crowds without winning ball games.

---

[15] Ibid.

Craig calls Montana a "Green Beret," undaunted in the pocket.[16] He believed in the system, his teammates and the play-call. He didn't rely too quickly or often on his own athleticism to try to rescue the day. He relied on those around him.

This level of trust isn't easy for everyone. Many are too afraid to trust. Some people can't let go of the notion, "If I want something done right, I have to do it myself." Others have been burned and their ability to entrust important matters to others has been crippled. In any case, **the organization is destined to remain small; forever subject to the ceiling of personal capacity.**

The essence of high-authorization leadership isn't about personal production or genius or brilliance. **High-authorization leadership is about collective achievement**—getting the team from here to there together. We can always accomplish more together than separately as disjointed individuals, no matter how gifted the individuals are. High-authorization leadership believes the common good will produce uncommon greatness. High-authorization leaders dare to believe in others.

So, Does This Mean We Quarterback by Committee?

While some creative processes can be well served by a collective think tank, I'm not suggesting a quarterback-by-committee leadership style. High-authorization leadership means finding the very best people available, placing them in significant, clearly defined roles and authorizing them to fill those roles—even to feel like *the quarterback* in that realm.

In his book, *Joy at Work,* Dennis Bakke suggests that a huge part of keeping people happy in the workplace

---

[16] Ibid.

is leading them to believe that their skills, insights and inputs are significant.

> Most senior executives seem to believe that God or the board created them to make all the important decisions. But every decision at headquarters takes away responsibility from people elsewhere in the organization and reduces the number of people who feel they are making an effective contribution to the organization. When central staffs assume the lion's share of power and control, the people who are operating units don't get as much excitement and fulfillment from their work.[17]

Bakke's common response to almost any question is, "What are your instincts telling you?" He then honors that viewpoint.

After hearing him speak at an engagement, I spoke with Bakke.

"What decisions do you make yourself?"

He didn't hesitate for even an instant before responding, "First, **I reserve the right to choose my closest associates.** Second, **I will not pass off to others the formation of core values** that drive the organization."

But beyond those fundamental decisions, Bakke **goes to great lengths *not* to go to great lengths.** In other words, he entrusts significant decisions — and imparts significance — to people around him. This, he says, fosters joy in the workplace more than fancy accoutrements and thin, fun-inducing gimmicks.

Level 4 vs. Level 5

So to some degree, the hyper-talented are at a

---

[17] Bakke, Dennis. *Joy at Work: A Revolutionary Approach to Fun on the Job.* Seattle: PVG, 2006.

disadvantage. Terribly talented and charismatic leaders (Jim Collins calls them "Level 4" leaders) have a hard time building sustainable success. Great at renewal and wonderful for inspiration, they tend to have difficulty sustaining success week after week. And they often lose the big games to the steady, less-talented, better-applied leaders—**sustaining leaders who are often as ordinary looking as they are smart ("Level 5" leaders).**

Like Bob Griese. As the quarterback for the 1972 Miami Dolphins, the only undefeated team in NFL history, Griese barely had the arm strength to hit his star receiver, Paul Warfield, in stride. But he was wise enough to hand the ball off to full-back Larry Csonka for the tough inside yards, and to Mercury Morris for mercurial outside yards. Only then, with the defense looking for the run, did Griese find his receivers open. The whole scheme made them the most dominant team ever, and turned their less-than-sensational but smart quarterback into a winning one.

Another Team Sport, Same Principle

Sport really does imitate life, especially team sports, since sustained success in life is rarely a singular experience. The other "ultimate team sport" is basketball, where the same principles hold true. Very few NBA scoring leaders have simultaneously won championships. In more than sixty years of record keeping, only Joe Fulks ('46-'47), George Mikan ('48-'49, '49-'50), Kareem Abdul-Jabbar ('70-'71) and Shaquille O'Neal ('99-'00) have accomplished this.

Oh, and then there's Michael Jordan. He did it *six times*.

Why so few championships for scoring leaders? **Big scorers, with the exception of Jordan, tend to try to *do too much*.** Jordan, unlike the dozens of other scoring leaders, also knew how to get the ball into the hands of others. His genius was clear. He knew that no one could single-cover him. So when they tried, he usually scored. When the double-team came, Jordan got the ball to other teammates--players he trusted, prodded and marshaled like few others. His career assist record (5.3 per game in the regular season and 5.7 per game in the playoffs) is impressive for a top scorer. And so are the rings on six fingers.

Other examples abound. Magic Johnson of the Lakers and Larry Bird of the Celtics battled for a decade, each with huge scoring potentials, but both committed to involving their teammates.

Oscar Robertson (Bucks and other teams) and Jerry West (Lakers) scored almost at will in previous decades, but chose to include their teammates in a total-team concept. Oscar actually *averaged* a triple-double for an entire season (ten or more points, rebounds and assists per game), a statistic that is every bit as monumental as Wilt Chamberlain's one hundred points in one game.

Wilt Chamberlain in his prime was an overpowering scoring machine. But even Wilt suffered defeat after defeat with the 76ers and Lakers when matched up against Bill Russell and the Boston Celtics. Russell's sense for team basketball is legendary and he filled fingers on both hands with rings. And when did Chamberlain finally win a championship? After seven consecutive scoring titles before 1966-67, Wilt lost the scoring crown while claiming his first of two league titles. Then, in his second title season, he didn't even lead his *team* in scoring.

In modern days, LeBron James and Kobe Bryant have both won championships and they've both won scoring titles. But neither has accomplished both feats in the same year. At the time of publication, Kevin Durant is the two-time consecutive scoring champ and his team hasn't enjoyed a league title.

My Personal Favorite

Growing up in the Pacific Northwest, my pick for the greatest *team* of all time is the 1977 Portland Trailblazers. Led by Bill Walton and a total-team system, the Blazers toasted the star-laden Philadelphia 76ers in the NBA finals with an awesome display of teamwork. The Blazers started two players (Bobby Gross and Dave Twardzik) who might not have started for any other team in the league. They weren't flashy or prone to generate points with one-on-one moves. But everyone knew their roles, trusted each other, passed, screened, moved without the ball and scored with staggering efficiency, and **beat teams with greater raw talent.**

Walton was a tremendous player in his prime, and proved when necessary that he could score almost at will. But most of the time, he willed his team to victories by drawing out the best in others.

So What Does This Mean?

My point is simply this: **the best leaders find ways to amplify the skills of associates by authorizing them to make significant contributions.** Like Tom Sawyer, athletes like Joe Montana, Michael Jordan and a short list of others have been able to empower associates and harness the best potentials for teamwork and excellence.

The first benefit of high-authorization leadership is that **the whole effort gains from the expertise and perspective** an able associate has to offer. People bring real value.

The second benefit is that the leader, by authorizing others, can reapply **energy and expertise to another emerging field** or to an ailing portion of the overall operation.

The third benefit is **morale**. Bright, competent people prefer to be respected. Giving them a real stake in the good of the organization makes pleasure in the workplace more likely. Morale affects quality, sustainability and longevity.

The fourth benefit of high-authorization is **replication**. By giving out real responsibility, we train and encourage emerging leaders who might end up replacing us effectively, or overseeing emerging divisions, or leading other worthy organizations.

One More Example from Sports

Watching the Blazers beat the 76ers was like watching the international teams beat the talented but hapless 2004 U.S. Olympic basketball team. As a big fan of teamwork and functional systems, I confess that I found myself overruling patriotism and rooting *against* the Americans. They played an uninspiring brand of ineffective basketball, virtually void of any visible system or the spirit that breeds success. They took turns hot-dogging and going one-on-one, ignoring fundamentals and getting beaten by less-talented, better-prepared teams. Unless the U.S. teams are composed of team-oriented role players who are committed to a winning system, we'll watch the U.S. teams get beat again in years to come. Since I'm not the only one to observe this reality, In fact, adjustments have already been made to our approach to team selection and strategy in the 2008 and 2012 Games.

A Leader: Someone People Follow, or Even...

One thing all leaders have in common is so completely obvious, and yet so awfully elusive. **Leaders turn around and see people following**; not grudgingly or under compulsion, but eagerly and fully engaged.

Sometimes followers are even alongside **or out ahead, feeling fully authorized and highly motivated.** While the notion of an associate getting out ahead can be foreign or threatening for some of us, it can also be revolutionary. Top-down, seniority-driven, turf-guarding models are more familiar to us, but not necessarily more effective. Our craving for the familiar—along with our fears of change—shouldn't prevent us from becoming a new and stronger type of leader. **People love to work for**—*actually with*—**leaders who are so generous and not in the least intimidated.**

A CEO in my circle of friends once worked in a huge, publicly traded, traditional, corporate structure with centralized staff and leadership. Up and down the line, staff were dissatisfied and the leadership was out of touch. While he observed dysfunction of every kind, he saw the fundamental problem at a national meeting of regional leaders. The national president gave a warm, affirming introduction of the corporate chair and mentioned "what a pleasure is it to work with him."

When the chair took the podium, he said in an all-too-serious way, "He got several things right in the introduction, but one thing was wrong. He doesn't work *with* me. He works *for* me."

Needless to say, that chair lost a ton of credibility for himself and millions of dollars for his company with that one careless comment—no, with that one arrogant self-disclosure. He revealed the tragic lack of soul in his organization and exposed the reason why he lost at least one—perhaps dozens or hundreds—of highly proficient executives.

One thing I forgot to mention about all those quarterbacks: **they had committed, voracious linemen blocking for them and believing in them—out ahead, running interference.** Those blockers went to hell and back to protect their quarterbacks and to promote their success. And those quarterbacks believed in their blockers enough to stand in the pocket, poised and confident, and deliver the ball to play-makers. And at the end of the game, with microphones and cameras blaring and flashing, the first thing the smart quarterback does is elevate the other players. "Man, I gotta give a shout-out to our line...they played an amazing game!"

When people feel respected, even empowered, trust and loyalty grow. Of course, loyalty can be bought, or even coerced. But trust can't. **A high-authorization culture is a high-trust environment.** And trust goes both ways; many ways, in fact. People believe in each other and practice doing things in ways that build and sustain mutual trust. That means relying on one another, as well as stepping up for each other. Some might even call this community.

Can I Become This Kind of Quarterback?

As I wrote the first draft of this chapter, the Patriots and Brady beat the Colts and Manning. I predicted similar outcomes for the future if things didn't change.

Things did change—for a while. Peyton Manning won his first Super Bowl. The Colts claimed the crown with a more balanced attack in a year when the quarterback didn't set any records. Something shifted. Was it stronger cast of players around the quarterback; more trust in each other?

Oh, and two more fascinating adds. First, when Peyton Manning got injured and sat out for an entire season in 2011, his team lost almost every game—he was far too central to his team's success.

Meanwhile, his younger brother Eli, a much less prodigious talent, won his second Super Bowl with the New York Giants in that same season, epitomizing the premise of this chapter and book.

Whitewashing the Fence

Chapter Four

Leadership as Coaching

Bobby **Knight is an intriguing study** in contrasts.

Knight retired from coaching basketball at Texas Tech, but is best known for his long tenure at Indiana University. On the one hand, some of his players rave about his integrity, work ethic and commitment to getting athletes through college. No one questions his knowledge of the game and few question his ability to lead—according to his own philosophy and style. Many respect Bobby Knight.

On the other hand, his rages and raving on-court antics have earned the disrespect of others. His micromanaging style, in concert with his verbal barrages, doesn't work for everyone. One former player represented the memories of many in a Sports Illustrated interview, saying that he wishes "people could really understand what it was like playing there or when things are going bad there that take away the enjoyment of the game… you get to the point where you are like, 'Screw this.' It just turns you off."[18]

Before critiquing Knight's leadership style, it's important to acknowledge that no leaders are perfect and that there are various personalities and approaches that can stimulate success.

That being said, Knight represents a leadership paradigm contrary to the premises of this book.

First, Knight's players **show every evidence of playing scared**. While his teams tend to be well-drilled, they often appear robotic, **as if the players are literally or virtually looking over their shoulders the entire game, afraid to displease.** This fear seems altogether warranted. Knight's outbursts are usually a barrage of accusations and have occasionally broken out into physicality that some would call abusive. "I think it is a demeaning, dehumanizing, debilitating type situation…constantly playing in fear."[19]

Second, the *kinds* of players who flourish under the Bobby Knights of the world tend to be **excellent followers and workers**, who thrive on clear-cut job descriptions and carefully enforced parameters.

There are exceptions. Isiah Thomas would be the most obvious. While at Indiana, this future Hall of Famer showed flashes of creativity and independence that characterized his long professional career. And Thomas, under Knight's coaching, won a national championship with Indiana.

Still, the ideal player under Knight is someone who takes orders and follows directions, military-style. Not everyone—especially the highly creative self-initiator—wants to play that game.

---

[18] Mandevile, Richard: *CNN-Sports Illustrated.com;* September 10, 2003.
[19] Donna, Gary: *CNN-Sports Illustrated.com;* September 10, 2003.

After a famous choking incident, another player on the team said, "If he touched me, it would have been all over the news, there would have been a fight. I would have ended up with a black eye and he would have ended up in the hospital."[20]

That brand of leadership can occasionally win championships for some coaches. Still, **the pool of truly talented players who thrive under the onslaught of verbal assault are few and far-between.** Even more, the bright, talented, self-initiating leader-type who would subject himself to someone like Knight is a rare bird. The list is long of significant players, including future stars at other schools and in the NBA, who walked away from Knight.[21]

I, for one, would never have played for Knight if I'd had major college basketball talent (I didn't). And I'd never let a son or daughter be coached by that style or philosophy. If someone like Knight had berated me, I like to think that I would have looked him straight in the eye and said, "If you can't treat me with respect, I can't respect you." Not everyone, of course, can choose out of a position under the influence of this leadership style and not everyone feels safe challenging heavy-handed authority.

Sometimes, with a coach or supervisor like this, it's necessary to rise up and stand against bad treatment. Yes, it might put us at risk of being *benched,* but it might also earn respect, help the supervisor and preserve the success of the organization. At the very least, it might make working conditions improve. And in other scenarios, leaving or being asked to leave could be the very best thing.

Always a leader among peers, and always respected by adults, my humble basketball game shriveled up and disappeared under Knight-like coaching. The screamers

---

[20] Ibid.
[21] Ibid.

and micromanagers just dried up my confidence, my natural bent toward creativity and my game.

In high school, one assistant coach was a screamer. In one game, under a barrage of micromanaging insults that were intended to improve me, I had the worst first half of my life. At halftime, another coach came and asked, "What's wrong?"

My answer was simple and mature for my age. **"When he's climbing all over me, I disappear. If he gets off my back, you'll see a totally different player emerge."**

The second assistant either went to the head coach with my appeal, or else he went directly to the screamer. Either way, the first assistant backed off and became more constructive with his coaching. I did emerge as a player. I felt more freedom, more respect and more confidence. I didn't question decisions as I made them or look over my shoulder to answer a constant flow of criticism. I did, by the way, respond to instruction, but not to tirades.

The same scenario played out in college. I went from being a two-point-per-game scrub to a scorer and leader on a small-college championship team. One component of the metamorphosis happened in seconds. The head coach simply asked the micromanaging assistant to back off. The head coach respected me, believed in me and accurately assessed the reality that I would respond better to less-controlling approaches to coaching. I literally went from a two-points-per-game reserve to a double-digit scorer and starter.

Another Kind of Coach

The greatest college basketball coach in history was John Wooden of UCLA. Testimonials, books and legends tell about a marvelous teacher who did most of his drilling in practice. His teams were very disciplined but obviously unafraid. While he was an active teacher in practice, Wooden's game-time approach was far more passive than most coaches. He handed them the ball and let them play the game.

Yes, he yelled at the players who responded to yelling. With all his players, **Wooden coaxed and prodded and taught and inspired according to their diverse temperaments and roles.** In the end, he said, if they weren't prepared, it was "my fault." If they won, it was "their victory." Here are some famous Wooden quotes:

> *A coach is someone who can give instruction without causing resentment.*

> *Consider the rights of others before your own feelings, and the feelings of others before your own rights.*

> *If you're not making mistakes, you're not doing anything. I'm positive that a doer makes mistakes.*

> *The main ingredient of stardom is the rest of the team.*[22]

That kind of coach **gets the best out of people.** And, equally important, that kind of coach *gets the best people*. The best players from all over the country clamored for the privilege of playing for John Wooden at UCLA. Lew Alcindor (later Kareem Abdul Jabbar) and Bill Walton are only two of the all-time greats who played for Wooden.

Smaller Spotlight, Same Scenario

My best coaches have been Wooden-types. Dave

---

[22] *Brainymedia.com*; 2008.

Lipp, long-time coach at Northwest Christian University in Eugene, Oregon, has a string of small-college and Bible-college national titles. My two years under Coach Lipp were his first two championship seasons.

Coach's goal was to raise up mature, faithful men, meld them into a family and do our best to represent God with excellence. And while we were at it, we won.

I joke to friends that we vicariously beat top-ranked Virginia. After all, Virginia was beaten by Chaminade of Hawaii in one of the great upsets in sports history. Chaminade was beaten by Concordia of Portland. And we beat Concordia of Portland. So we could have beaten Virginia, right? Well, even our talented 6'5" center would have had a tough matchup against Virginia's 7'4"All-American, Ralph Sampson. We all would have been overmatched.

Still, Coach Lipp was a person-builder, more prone to bench us for outbursts of childish behavior than for turnovers or miscues. **He knew that he was teaching life, not just a game**. His greater goal was the development of our character. Still, being a fierce competitor, Coach Lipp also knew that people of strong character are more likely to join and create a winning team.

There's a Place for the Yellers

Most teams hire assistants to play the bad-cop role—conditioning and discipline. Sometimes, yelling gets the point across. If we can't handle a good dressing-down on occasion, then we'd better toughen up.

I tested my core premises in this chapter with Hall of Fame football star, Ronnie Lott. As a friend and an active partner in my work, Ronnie is a great go-to guy. In this case, he reacted to my critique of Bobby Knight by saying, "I always responded well to the screamers. They got it out of me. Fear of failure in their eyes inspired me to improve." Knowing Ronnie's monumental toughness, his reaction doesn't surprise me. And I respect his reality and instincts.

Still, I suggest that Ronnie is an exception, just as his career and ongoing approach to life are exceptional.

As a whole, the best kind of leadership is about respect. The best people have so many choices, including the choice to opt out of experiences that are unpleasant or demeaning. Of course, not everyone can walk away from an unsatisfying employment situation. But the best people usually can. And those are the ones I want to recruit and keep.

Even for less-proven talents, the prospect of bringing out their best work would suggest that we test our models and find what works best. People do their best work in a context of mutual respect.

In today's society, for better or worse, respect is no longer a positional grant. Respect is earned, not dictated. The best coaches and leaders **earn respect by** *modeling* **respect**. Leaders and institutions that are bossy, cold and hierarchical are simply bad for people, bad for business and bad for our community. They also fail to draw the brightest, most creative talent. And if they draw the talent, they can't *keep* it.

Even if controllers and screamers succeed here or there, they are contributing much less to the common good—a society of decency and respect—than the Woodens of the world.

Leader as Coach

Whatever the organization, the leader is the coach. His or her spirit, tone, style, and philosophy will permeate the entire organization. **Look at your leadership circle today and you're sneaking a peek at your entire organization in five years**—less than five years, in some cases.

Coaches and leaders teach, inspire, correct, prune, reward and shape an entire culture—for better or worse. As Tony Dungy, former coach of the Indianapolis Colts, writes in his book, *Quiet Strength*:

> What will people remember us for? Are other people's lives better because we lived? Did we make a difference? ...significance doesn't show up in won-loss records, long resumes, or the trophies on our mantels. It's found in the hearts and minds of those we've come across who are in some way better because of the way we lived.[23]

The best coaching is about respect for that process and stewarding a sacred trust—our influence.

High-authorization leadership is about respect and high levels of trust. High-authorization leadership empowers people by granting real authorization. Then it gives the freedom and space to **allow others to put their own signature on the roles they play** and the contributions they make. Yes, it still involves clear information about hopes and expectations on the part of the leader, and even strong, honest accountability. But it's more Wooden than Knight, more Level 5 than Level 4, more Montana than Marino, more Reagan than Carter and, for the best of motives, a bit of Tom Sawyer. Tom inspired interest, equipped his friends for success, communicated with clarity what needed to be done, and then *let them do it.*

So, in the spirit of John Wooden**, let 'em play**. Let go of the need to micromanage. Get rid of the ball, the ego and the need to do too much. Put the ball in the hands of people who can make plays and trust them enough to live, serve and excel with a freer hand.

[23] Dungy, Tony. *Quiet Strength: The Principles, Practices, & Priorities of a Winning Life.* Carol Stream, Il: Tyndale, 2007.

This means, of course, hiring people who *can* make plays. In this high-authorization model, **I'm looking for people who don't need much hand-holding or many forceful directives.** I'm after people who enjoy responsibility, know how to get the most out of a team and can naturally infuse the whole organization with the values that drive us. It's not always about getting better people. The key is finding the ones who *fit:* trusting and trustworthy people who are free-thinking and willing to let others enjoy real responsibility.

Going back to basketball imagery, I'm looking for savvy point-guards who control the tempo, spread the ball around, get everyone involved and aren't afraid of both worthy structure and needful innovation.

Of course, we also need shooting-guards—the people who can sink the shot, close the deal, score the winning basket. We need strong, steady centers who anchor the organization. And we need agile, small forwards who are versatile enough to fill various roles. And I love a burly power forward who sets strong picks, plays imposing defense and makes other players look even better than they are.

But you hear the basketball prognosticators say it throughout the month of March, during the "madness" of the college basketball championships: **"It's the point-guards that make all the difference, now that it's crunch time."**

Basketball aside, Tom Sawyer was no tyrant and the force of his leadership was joy, persuasion and a shrewd understanding of his peers. We simply have to know that the best and most sustainable way to lead others is not by ranting and raving. There's a better way. A *much* better way.

That's what I'm looking for—a **savvy person who loves to involve, inspire and fully authorize others**.

Basketball players say it out loud all the time. "I love to play with a point-guard like that."

So as a leader or coach, be a person like that.

Even more, look for people like that. The other thing people say about a great point-guard? **"It's like having another coach on the floor."** In other words, we're looking to recruit leaders who can spread our values throughout the entire organization.

Chapter Five

The Greatest Leader of All

The most tantalizing and obvious example of high-authorization leadership is Jesus. This central figure of the Christian faith has influenced world history more than any other person. Any attempt to catalog the monumental influence of Jesus would either be long and tedious or thin and unsatisfactory. Jesus changed the world.

What was His Leadership Strategy?

Not much is known about Jesus the carpenter before his days as a preacher and healer. But when the time comes to go public, Jesus chooses twelve people from among the many who follow and listen to him. These become known as the "apostles", or messengers.

About seventy others, women and men, stay nearby, listening and learning and modeling their lives after the worldview and agenda of Jesus. These are his "disciples" or apprentices.

Beyond the "twelve" and the "seventy" are the multitudes, or crowds. Curiosity seekers and antagonists jockey with the sick and the lame to get close to him. Everyone wants to be near this truth-teller, who brings help and renewal to people suffering in body and soul. They want to hear his stories, touch his clothes and draft on his eternal hope.

For three years he pours himself into his closest associates, imparting values and modeling behaviors. He sends them out for trial runs and educational experiences. He gradually increases their responsibilities. Once, Jesus launches them out in pairs and authorizes them to do the same things he would do, and with the authority of his own name. They have some highs and some lows, but come back to Jesus fully engaged with stories and more questions about how to do the work.

Among the crowds, Jesus makes many friends and gathers multitudes of admirers. But his greatest investment of time and leadership is in mentoring his closest associates.

And **then he leaves, putting the enterprise in the hands of an eclectic crew of fishermen, tax collectors, prostitutes and widows.**

There's so much more to be said about Jesus' specific teachings, as well as the extraordinary claims surrounding his identity and last days on earth. But the purpose of this book is to offer a clear, compelling model for leaders.

Jesus' model is a high-authorization approach that gives away real authority and actual responsibility while building genuine partnership. Jesus leaves the fledgling business of helping and saving the world in the hands of ordinary people. People say they believe in Jesus? Jesus believes in people!

Jesus' Core Values and Clear Vision

There are **three core teachings** that form the basic philosophy of Jesus, found in the first four books of the New Testament of the Bible.

1.   **The Greatest Commandment**: *"Love the Lord your God with all your heart and with all your soul and with all your mind...and love your neighbor as yourself."*[24]

2.   **The Golden Rule**: *"So in everything, do unto others what you would have them do unto you, for this sums up the Law and the Prophets."*[25]

3.   **The Great Commission**: *"All authority in heaven and on earth has been given to me. Therefore go and make disciples of all nations, baptizing them in the name of the Father and of the Son and of the Holy Spirit, and teaching them to obey every thing I have commanded you. And surely I am with you always, to the very end of the age.*[26]

The Great Commission serves as a **mission statement** for the emerging organization, which has become the largest in the history of the world. The first sentence is critical. Jesus understands his influence and the authority that's been given to him. Even in his most humble moments, he doesn't deny the importance of his role or pretend that the whole helping effort can happen without him. In the following excerpt from his story, we see both

---

[24] *Matthew* 22:37
[25] *Matthew* 7:12
[26] *Matthew* 18:20

his sense of authority and his strategic philosophy for changing the world:

> *Jesus knew that the Father had put all things under his power, and that he had come from God and was returning to God; so he got up from the meal, took off his outer clothing, and wrapped a towel around his waist. After that, he poured water into a basin and began to wash his disciples' feet, drying them with the towel that was wrapped around him.... "Now, I have set you an example that you should do as I have done for you."*[27]

Jesus' leadership model is to serve and empower his associates, and not from a self-concept of inferiority. He proclaims his life ethic when he says he *"did not come to be served but to serve. . . ."*[28] Jesus wasn't hung up on his authority.

Go and Make Disciples

Jesus only exercised his public leadership for three years. He proved most determined to give the ongoing work to his associates.

"Now go," said Jesus, *"and make disciples of all nations...."* Jesus' own efforts are staged mostly in Israel, with a few episodes across the borders. Now the work would go international and Jesus wasn't the one to franchise it out. Those previously provincial apprentices

---

[27] *John* 13:1-5, 15
[28] *Matthew* 20:28

would be agents of real change that would spread to the whole earth.

He taught them to baptize—which means immerse—and teach. Both are critical. We who lead need to **immerse people in a culture of commitment and community and teach the core values and critical behaviors that drive the success of the enterprise.**

For example, staff meetings are critical opportunities to reiterate the driving values of the organization with so much repetition that all executives can do the same with their own teams. Every leadership culture needs to assess frequency of meetings and then use those sessions to infuse core values and reinforce critical behaviors. The specific agenda and contents of those meetings might change from season to season, reflecting organizational needs and group energy levels, but the goal is the same—**make sure we're all on the same page in the crucial areas of values, vision, strategies, goals and—in some cases—tactics.**

Why do I say "…in some cases…?" Because I'm not going to impose my tactical approach on everyone. If I've enlisted extraordinary leaders, I also impart some freedom for them to put their own signatures on the way their pieces of the organization operate.

Yes, there are some tactics that are common to all "divisions." And there has to be some accountability between divisions, since each is interdependent on the other. I usually open the floor of meetings in a way that allows each executive team member to exercise accountability toward one another—and me—and to cross-pollinate with ideas and tactics. I recommend Patrick Lencioni's book, *The Five Dysfunctions of a Team*[29] to cultivate a culture that celebrates healthy conflict and draws

---

[29] Lencioni, Patrick. *The Five Dysfunctions of a Team: A Leadership Fable.* San Francisco: Jossey-Bass, 2002.

out constructive criticism of one another. Leadership cultures have to grow away from the habit of *niceness* that can hamper good communication and honest accountability. Contrary to popular notions, Jesus wasn't always nice.

Honesty leads to authentic community and a functional team. It cuts away the stifling effects of politics, unites the different divisions and programs and opens the door to deeper trust and universal excellence.

Still, each team member uses tactics that fit his or her own personality, expertise and field of operation. While people have to be able to question and challenge one another, we also must respect each other.

But core values and certain critical behaviors must be universally owned within the organization. If we build the house without a set of foundational, agreed-upon core values, it's like building a house on a fault line. Trouble, and even triumph, can shake and break the house. Things will come apart.

Jesus knew this. So he preached sermons, told stories and modeled behaviors repeatedly in ways that immersed his associates with the core values and driving behaviors that were vital for future success.

Jesus Did Not Abdicate

Before his physical departure, as the capstone to the Great Commission, Jesus said, "And surely I am with you always, to the very end of the age."[30] Christians believe that Jesus never *really* left. His "spirit", teachings and stories remain for study and application. He hasn't abdicated. He hasn't abandoned.

In the development of this leadership model, **I was often guilty of abdication.** While it was good to give team

---

[30] *Matthew* 28:20b

members freedom and real authority, at times I let leaders fail for too long before intervening. And in other cases, I allowed so much autonomy that the different programs grew apart. Some call this the *silo effect,*[31] where disconnected towers of influence grow up and away from each other; each doing good work, but in disconnected ways.

I'm learning how important it is to stay involved, primarily through relationships. And I also champion an annual or seasonal goal that has compelling implications for every program and binds us together around common values, visions, goals and strategies.

So we can't walk away, or be too distant, aloof or uninvolved. **I don't want to micromanage, but I still need to be present, available, and consistent** about communicating the messages that unite every department.

Still, "It's Your Baby"

Jesus has authorized the twelve, and even a larger set of interested apprentices, to go and make things happen—teach, heal, love, confront, advocate, restore, reconcile, give and serve. Jesus has essentially said, "It's your baby. I'm not really gone, but it's in your hands. If you fail, you have my grace. If you succeed, you have my gratitude. So go, build the organization. Live the life I've modeled and taught. Take the product (love, hope, joy, peace, faith) on the road." Jesus said, "You will be my representatives in ever-widening circles of influence."[32] And Jesus believes in the products and services of the organization as if he, and then they, are "the light of the world."[33]

---

[31] Lencioni, Patrick. *Silos, politics and Turf Wars: A Leadership Fable About Destroying the Barriers That Turn Colleagues Into Competitors.* San Francisco: Jossey-Bass, 2006.
[32] *Acts* 1:8

It will forever seem ludicrous that something as critical as the salvation of the world would be placed in frail human hands. But that's the intrigue of the Christian story: people try to trust God, while God entrusts people with the most consequential work imaginable.

It's outrageous and wonderful — a model of leadership that pronounces worth and establishes purpose, even as it guards the dignity of human personality.

Tell Them, Show Them, Let Them

The strategy is simple. Pour energy into select people, teach core values and model critical behaviors. Tell them, show them and *let them*. Authorize those key associates to do "all things in my name, and even greater things shall you do than I have done."[34] Send them, but in **a high-grace culture where aggressive failures are rewarded more than safe passivity**.

I often tell my teammates, "I'd rather have you fall forward than fall backward. Take risks. Experiment with innovations. You can make forgivable mistakes in strategy and tactics that might hurt for a season; but adopt my values and commit to the core behaviors that will sustain us and grow us in any season."

Using a parable as a teaching tool, Jesus equates the whole enterprise to a man going on a journey. He delegates the care of the organization to three people. The first manages aggressively and to good effect, relinquishing assets to others and investing with risk. The second also takes risks and sees results. Afraid of the boss's wrath, the third agent is protective, fearful and possessive, burying his assets under his own care with no good effect. And he suffers the strong rebuke of the boss. Jesus teaches a

---

[33] *Matthew* 5: 14,16
[34] *John* 14:12

vigorous, courageous approach to fully invested leadership and celebrates anyone who "believes" enough to do things his way—a robust, adventurous way.[35]

Many of Jesus' stories are about trust. The owner of the vineyard leaves, but he's coming back. He leaves people a trust along with the full authorization to apply it well. What account will the fully-authorized steward report when the owner returns?

Jesus is clearly determined to raise up purposeful risk-takers with a heart for teamwork and a set of values bigger than those of the individual.

The same could be true even of the best for-profit companies—there's an ethic that's bigger than the bottom line. **Profit will be a byproduct of widespread clarity and adherence to core values and critical behaviors that make a service or product attractive and effective.**

The greatest leaders teach, preach, model, persuade and enlist "disciples" who embrace those values and practice those critical behaviors—and convince others to do the same.

This might be the only time you see Jesus' and Steve Jobs' names in the same sentence, but the correlation is clear in this case. As I type this book into an Apple MacBook Pro, the instrument has all the markings of a leader absolutely committed to a vision of both function and artistry. Barely ever nice, Steve Jobs was passionate about "teaching, preaching, modeling, persuading and enlisting disciples" who shared his passion for devices that would outshine the opponents' in both design and precision. Mission accomplished.

Comparing Jesus to Tom Sawyer can also be an *apples-to-oranges* fiasco. The fundamental difference—motive—is so completely obvious that it seems silly to try to reconcile the two icons.

---

[35] *Matthew* 25:14-30

But there are obvious commonalities. Both are able to enlist and inspire others to do things that those people would otherwise be shy about doing. And Jesus and Tom are able to leave the primary work in the hands of highly engaged people so both can move on to other frontiers.

Chapter Six

Tending the Garden

As Jesus paints word pictures of the core values and chief strategies that define his movement, he uses organic images of soil, seed and plant. Yes, it's strategic in a first-century agrarian society to speak in familiar terms. But the picture still works today. Great leaders know that the best organizations are **growing, breathing, feeding, spreading organisms. They're alive.**

And then there are institutions—relatively immobile and so often lifeless. There are, of course, many great institutions. But the best ones defy the impulse to behave like one:

Institutions are fixed and inflexible.
Organic structures are mobile and fluid.

For *institutions,* change is suspect.
For *organisms,* change is the norm.

Institutions "fear the shear."
Organisms know that pruning stiff, rigid
structures is actually safer for the organism than
protective, preservationist behavior.

Institutions focus on old things like legacy and
heritage while celebrating the past.
Organisms foster new life and celebrate the future.

Institutions are bigger than people, use people and
treat people like interchangeable parts.
Organisms ARE people and they know that
relationship matters more than hierarchy; function
matters more than form; health more than history;
people more than programs.

There are numerous ways to strategize, but the best organic strategies are **relationally aggressive**. While structures, hierarchies and forms have function, those constructs are only useful to the degree that they facilitate meaningful relationship. As one associate used to remind me, **"Structures and programs are only hangers for relationship."**

The Problem with Guardians

Even the history of successful, long-established organizations can be a curse. History is only helpful as it instructs the present and future. Living in the past is impossible, therefore inadvisable. As futurist Eddie Gibbs writes,

> The longer a person lives, the more he or she tends to dwell on the past rather than live in dynamic interaction with the present or be inspired by the hope of future possibilities. If

this is true for the individual, it also holds true for institutions that have inherited corporate culture reinforced by each succeeding generation.

Furthermore, when changes in society are occurring at a rapid rate and in an unpredictable manner, the desire to resort to protective entrenchment becomes stronger.[36]

So we need leaders who are willing to break out of institutional mindsets, protective shells and traditional behavior. We need people in key positions who are innovative and courageous. And **those who oversee them must allow enough space, support and protection for innovators to really shake things up—and then reward them.**

The best organizations—those that reach more people in more life-changing ways—are in a perpetual state of flux. Not in their core values and not in their primary vision. But the best organizations are living the ethic of Paul, an early Christian innovator, "to become all things to all men so that by all possible means I might save some."[37] Versatility and the ability to adapt to changing circumstances are crucial.

If I'm going to enlist, support and sustain those kinds of leaders—innovative, courageous, curious people—I need to let them flourish in a high-authorization culture.

The Safest Road to Success: Innovation

In taking a personality test, I discovered that I'm a high conformity type. In other words, according to

---

[36] Gibbs, Eddie. *Church Next: Quantum Changes in How We do Ministry.* Downers Grove, IL: InterVarsity Press, 2000.
[37] I *Corinthians* 9:22

core temperament I'm prone to be a guardian of traditions and protocol. I'm naturally protective of the legacy of organizations and I'm less likely to be an innovator. Proven methodologies appeal to me and time-tested approaches to life and leadership tend to compel me more than "the latest thing." I've been a slow adapter to technologies and a slow adopter of new-fangled approaches.

While **leaders come in many temperament types,** my type comes with the inherent risk of protectionist behavior. My knee-jerk instinct is to resist innovation.

But what I'm learning is that an organic, high-authorization culture requires a leader who honors innovation. Granting real authority means allowing space for curious, brave people to initiate worthy innovation. If the chief executive is actually a guardian of health, **what is the safest way to guard the health of the organization? Make sure that it's organic**—creative, innovative and alive—rather than stiff and institutional. **The most dangerous way to live, personally or collectively, is out of fear.** We can't be afraid of change.

So it sounds like double-talk, but here it is: If you want to be a guardian of the health and future of your organization, then stand careful guard over the innovators while they make their radical, invasive, obtrusive and altogether life-breathing suggestions.

In helping and visiting churches, I've seen the musty sanctuaries of hundreds of near-empty churches where change-resistance has led to obsolescence, marginalization and deterioration. These places are like museums regaling past victories in long-ago seasons. They're like discarded shells on the beach that once housed living organisms and now only decorate communities like windowsill ornaments.

Again, as a "guardian" by nature, I refuse to let misguided guardians of the church harm her future. **With the notable exception of corruption—which can scorch**

any organization like wildfire--classic, guardian behavior is the biggest deterrent to progress in the church. Core values that make us credible must be timeless, changeless and safely guarded. But **one of those "guarded" values must be a commitment to innovation.**
Any leader of any organization would be wise to guard against stiff, change-resistant institutionalism.

Hire Innovators and Help Them Succeed

So I hire innovators and authorize them to do what they do. And **I provide for them and protect them in their courageous work**
For example, I once worked with an energetic, innovative youth pastor charged with reigniting a youth program that had lost some steam. Among other things, he started taking a handful of teens to Mexico to build simple, useful homes during Spring break. Over time, he invited the entire church to come along. Year by year, the numbers grew, until we peaked at more than two hundred people in one year—including a hundred high school students—from small children to eighty-year-olds making the pilgrimage. Over the years, more than eight hundred different people have traveled to Mexico for that annual trek. He didn't just grow the youth program. He revolutionized the church!
It wasn't my idea and I wasn't in charge. In fact, in years when I joined the trip, I made it very clear to my associate that I would "only wear my boss hat" when he specifically asked me to. Otherwise, I was "one more strong back to haul cement," laughing with the pleasure of seeing quality leadership and the overall effects on the wider organization.

Vicarious Pleasure is a Great Thing

It's so fun to see people thrive and jive with

enthusiasm and creativity. I get juiced by seeing associates succeed in a context that allows them freedom to actually, completely lead.

I relish this process even more than Tom Sawyer. While Tom sees the successful enlistment of others as a chance to goof off under a tree, I see their success as my freedom to catalyze change on another frontier. And then I eventually pass that new work off to a whole new set of strong, inspired leaders.

The opposite approach is stiff and controlling. It assumes that the best ideas flow downhill from my own genius or from the collective genius of the gallery of leaders hanging on the portrait wall outside the corner office. Those "great" ideas roll down the hall to underlings, incapable of bringing value beyond their ability to follow orders.

That approach might be useful in some organizations, but it does not produce the yield we want in most cases.

Freedom as a Driving Value

This high-authorization model is driven by **a tenacious respect for human freedom**.

At least two influences drive my commitment to freedom. First, my parents nurtured their kids in "preparatory" ways, more than "protective" ways and fostered a band of pretty strong, high-achieving kids. Second, my worldview includes the notion that **God's biggest daily miracle is restraint**. As tempting as it might be to make liberal use of a divine thumb, squelching every outbreak of idiocy, instead *divine restraint* invites people to find creative and heroic solutions to our crises—however self-inflicted.

Freedom is necessary for the human experience to be authentic and not robotic. I can appreciate the fact that my vacuum cleaner obeys me every time I push the button, but I do not love my vacuum cleaner or expect great things from it. On the other hand, my children have free will and do not always obey; but I *love them* and revel in the moments when they succeed at noble things—**especially when they reach new heights born out of their imagination and determination.**

Just as there is danger in turning my children into rule-keepers instead of independent problem-solvers, there is danger in making organizations rigid, rule-bound or subject to heavy-handed leadership.

So this high authorization, high respect, high trust model of leadership is about helping the organism flourish. And it helps me flourish, since the same measure of heavy-handed judgment and control that I pour out will be poured out on me. I want to create a culture where others succeed around me by being more completely themselves: **busy doing what they love with freedom and passion**, with little institutional resistance or overbearing supervision.

Yet they are accountable to partners, fellow enthusiasts and interested investors in their potentials. And they're accountable to me. They do not work alone. They have each other to cross-pollinate, refine and reinforce each other in a setting that feels like community. And they have me, affirming and protecting them. They do not suffer the weight of my stern, oppressive gaze very often. They know what they'll get from me and I usually know what I'll get from them: respect and a hunger for excellence.

At the end of day, it all feels strangely like *whitewashing the fence.* I don't mean that I laze around under the tree while others do the work. I *do* mean that I watch with enormous vicarious pleasure as they excel to their hearts' desires.

Organic, creative, innovative leaders must have a field of play. People simply work harder and respond better when they want to be there. And nothing steals morale faster than labor at the hands of a tyrant. A smart executive hires and authorizes people who can cultivate a context for dynamic and purposeful change.

The Natural Flow

Most new enterprises go through a metamorphosis:

Movement > organism > organization > institution

That *last* move is the precursor to death. With institutionalization comes calcification. Calcified organizations constrict innovators, respond slowly to cultural shifts, lose the capacity to engage and inspire and eventually fade away.

If we care about the future of our ventures, we will infuse life and resist calcification. We will keep growing, experimenting and risking, sometimes against a current of cautious voices.

By the way, Collins' "Level-4 leaders" are usually experts at breaking up calcification and restoring organic health. The Level-4 leader is the classic re-igniter, turning around organizations by pruning dry shoots and boldly fostering new life, often by the force of personality.

But even then comes the question of sustaining health. Collins celebrates "Level-5 leaders [who] set up their successors for even greater success in the next generation, whereas egocentric Level-4 leaders often set up their successors for failure."[38] How do Level 5 leaders sustain success? Mostly by empowering others.

Whitewashing the Fence is about both transforming cultures and sustaining health. Leadership cultures become healthy, and then remain healthy, when brave innovators are empowered. In fact, a dynamic tension permeates

---

[38] Collins, Jim. *Good to Great.* New York: HarperCollins, 2001.

meetings and cascades out. People aren't afraid to do the hard thing, ask the tough question, challenge each other to think and rethink strategies and tactics and even prune. **Brittle and lifeless forms are sacrificed to make room for newer and better ways to emerge.** Champions are free and protected to do these often-emotional tasks.

Years ago, my family moved into a home with an old, raspy plant spiking up out of the back garden. No blooms and no shoots; just brown, empty sticks giving no evidence of life or nurture. On the verge of digging it out, I asked a friend what to do.

"Cut it down almost to the ground, and fresh shoots will spring up."

"What is it?" I asked.

"Just wait. It'll come back. You'll see."

I waited. When I was about to give up, fresh sprouts emerged out of the roots; not out of the stiff, hollow shoots. The green overtook the brown and engulfed the chimney, wall and eaves. Then the most amazing purple blooms exploded on the scene. An amazing bougainvillea almost engulfed the house!

I still had to groom often and prune each year. The plant presented far more trouble than the old brown clump of nothing. But it was alive and beautiful.

Pruning is emotional work. It always feels risky. And even those hollow shoots once served well! Should I really sacrifice those aging forms for the sake of emerging life? Not always, perhaps. After all, I didn't dig out the whole plant. But honest, hard work had to be done or else the once-lively organism ran the risk of being a mere shell of its former self.

Whitewashing the Fence

SECTION TWO

A Culture Altering Strategy

Whitewashing the Fence

Chapter Seven

Authorization: It's Your Baby

The obvious practice of high-authorization leadership is this: granting a high level of authority to competent people. Using Roger Craig's comment about Joe Montana, it's "getting rid of the ball quickly and putting it in the hands of people who can make plays."

This means telling associates, even volunteers, "It's your baby. I won't be meddling or micromanaging. I won't even give you ideas unless you ask for them. This is your program to run, your division to build, your team to lead."

Getting to the practice of truly authorizing others takes enormous humility. Jim Collins says that lesser leaders are "people who could never in a million years bring themselves to subjugate their egoistic needs for the greater ambition of building something longer and more lasting than themselves."[39]

We have to be humble enough to hire and empower people who are *more* competent than we are in particular areas. I can't be bothered or threatened by fellows who are true stars in their fields. And if there is a portion of the broad work that no one can perform to my competence level, then I have to ask myself some hard questions:

- Do I continue to do the bulk of the work in that area?

- Do I hire someone who can act on my directives (a manager more than a self-initiating leader)?

- Do I hire someone less competent and learn to bite my tongue and allow that person autonomy even if that person can't live up to my standard?

- Or, do I hire an apprentice with great potential so I can coach and mentor that person toward high-level competence?

I prefer to coach and mentor in those instances, though each choice might have merit in different circumstances.

Authorization Does Not Mean Abdication

Authorization does not mean abdication. It doesn't mean we lose interest or disappear altogether. It doesn't mean we abandon our associates or create too much distance.

---

[39] Collins, Jim. *Good to Great.* New York: HarperCollins, 2001.

Sometimes, I've abdicated. Why? In some cases, I disappeared because I was so confident in the associate's vision and ability. Other times, I abdicated because other arms of the enterprise hijacked my interest. In still other cases, I was in a season of fatigue that simply required others to exist and proceed without enjoying much help from me.

Whatever the cause, I'm learning that it's costly when authorization tips over into abdication. Our associates will either feel abandoned or they'll want for accountability—or both.

Follow Through

Some strong associates are granted authorization only to have it withdrawn later. That *bait and switch* leads to real confusion and frustration.

Or they work autonomously to great effect and then watch while their supervisors get all the credit and rewards. This can lead to bitterness.

Or they've been told they have freedom to fail boldly and then, when failing, have taken the greater share of the blame. "But you said you wanted me to live on the edge!"

The best leaders absorb blame and share credit, not vice versa.

Later chapters will deal with the best kinds of protection so that high authorization doesn't lead to confusion and disappointment. Without such assurances, there will be no trust.

Trust is a Must

First and foremost, high-authorization leadership requires trust. The leader must trust the associate to have the competency and commitment to deliver excellent products and services. And the associate needs to trust that the leader will not be unfair, unappreciative or insincere about offering real responsibility.

Imparting trust is hard for some people. By nature, some personalities are naturally dominant, highly directive and have great difficulty delegating any real authority to others. As I've written earlier, this isn't all bad. But these micro-managers often serve best in management roles where the product or service is actually produced by temperament types who prefer clean, concrete direction. **If people who have difficulty trusting others serve at higher levels, they will attract and keep fewer innovative and creative types,** who often scream and run for the hills under heavy management. And again, we'll end up stifling growth and creativity, acting as bottlenecks to our own higher hopes.

If we're in executive leadership, we want to hire leaders—strong self-starters, creative minds, entrepreneurial spirits. Those kinds of people shrivel up and die at the hands of micromanagers. Or else they just go away and join a competing enterprise—or start one. Micromanagers kill strong, self-initiating leaders.

In my non-profit efforts, these principles were doubly true. Micromanaging executives attract people who love to be highly directed—even commanded. **Some people like to be told exactly what to think and do, without room for ambiguity or personal interpretation.** While some of these colonies of same-thinkers can be huge, streamlined and productive, they can also be susceptible to every kind of abuse and manipulation.

Most of these organizations are not huge or productive, since the overall service is limited to the scope and vision of the micromanaging leader. Too many executives micromanage others until the potential leaders are disenfranchised and the work force dwindles down to the workers who love clean and clear job descriptions, following directions and taking orders.

For example, the back rows of churches are loaded with stronger lay leaders whose enormous potentials lie dormant *only at church*. They aren't enlisted, inspired, respected or unleashed to express their God-given gifts with freedom and authority.

Most top-level executives can recollect a time when a board tried to manage the CEO too tightly—without trust. When that happens, the organization will either frustrate strong creative CEOs or attract CEOs who lack the confidence to truly lead. **Micromanaging boards kill strong, gifted CEOs and chase away capable leaders. We can do the same thing to our associates.**

I knew an executive who hired an associate when the organization reached a size and sophistication that required more leadership. He absolutely did not trust his talented new associate. So he spent the next two years withholding and stripping real authority from that associate, until the associate dried up and finally left. The organization began to shrink and even the leader walked away exhausted. Everyone suffered.

In that case, I didn't see the executive as non-coachable or incurably controlling. He just needed to trust someone. A good mentor—or even a good book—might have helped the executive change his ways, trust his associate, enlarge his influence and further the organization.

Sometimes, Distrust is all About the Associate

There are cases when an associate is not trustworthy, either because of a character flaw, a lack of sufficient skill or negligent levels of commitment. Toward that reality, the first step to a high-authorization culture is to **enlist the right people.** As Collins puts it, "Get the right people on the bus." This means finding people of credible character, healthy commitment and considerable competence. Collins writes, **"The moment you feel the need to tightly manage someone, you've made a hiring mistake."**[40]

Finding the best people requires us to swim in streams that are producing great people—the right schools or organizations or mentoring circles. It also means using hiring processes that draw out character issues, not just skill, experience or intellect.

Then we must give people roles that match and ignite their skills and passions. **People usually** *do best* **what they** *enjoy most.* **People usually** *enjoy most* **what they** *do best.* And **people also tend to flourish in roles where they've played a part in crafting the job description.** While every job has components that are pure hard work, most people would prefer roles that require the greater percentage of focus and energy in realms of enjoyment and giftedness. As Collins writes, once you have the right people on the bus, make sure they're sitting in the right seats—doing what they love and excelling at it.

Grow Up Some Apprentices

I try to have at least one trainee (usually several) who is hired more for potential than for measurable competence. Sometimes these are people within the organization who show leadership promise and need to be tried and tested. Other times, we find trainees in schools or related fields. Even if these developing leaders can't produce at the same level as tested leaders, training these people is part of my contribution to the broader good. I assume that we'll eventually launch these folks into other fields, or let them advance into positions of greater trust in

---

[40] Ibid.

our organization. Those **trainees are given increasing levels of trust, responsibility and authority as they grow and prove themselves.** As Jesus teaches in Matthew 25:21 of the Bible, *those who are faithful with little will be given much.* As any smart executive knows, if we can find quality people, we need to hand them real responsibility and give them all they need to succeed.

But **mostly, we look for the very best we can find in their fields after wide-sweeping searches.** Sometimes, limited money limits the scope of our search. Other times, we need to hire quickly and so our search is regional or within the organization. But even then, we're hoping for people who really can do the job.

If I can entrust the work to a qualified person, then the scope of my influence grows.

Sometimes, Distrust is About Me

If I can't trust the best people, then the problem is me. I'm having a hard time letting go of control.

Why can it be hard to let go?

Sometimes, **we overestimate our own skills** or knowledge. We steal freedom and pleasure from other competent people and we rob the organization of their brilliance.

Or **we overestimate our own time and energy capacities** and become bottlenecks, sabotaging our own high hopes by creating logjams on our own desks. The growth of the organization is stunted by our limitations of time, energy and attention.

Sometimes, we're truly afraid to authorize and **our fearful behaviors permeate the culture with caution** that douses the flames of creativity and stifles the risky behavior necessary to be a breakout enterprise.

Or in other cases, authorizing associates is

counterintuitive because of basic temperament. For example, the workaday, problem-oriented, melancholic beaver rarely makes a great executive leader. The impulsive paranoia ("Water is pouring over the dam! Everything is coming apart!") will simply paralyze a team or distract people into perpetual maintenance and repair modes.

Of course, problem solving is good. The dam always needs some repair. But a few beavers can be hired and fully authorized to repair imperfections quietly, while high-level leaders are venturing out more boldly. The entire organization cannot be subjected to that level of vigilance. You are an architect of change, not an engineer of small improvements. Someone else can manage improvements. You need to inspire real innovation and courageous movement.

Improvement is a Tempting Snare

Most often, we make the mistake of thinking, "If I can walk around helping to improve everyone's efforts, then the whole will be enlarged." In actuality, by meddling, we will sometimes chase away the people who can do the work *better* than we can. **If I can improve the work of an associate, then it usually means I've hired the wrong person.**

Or it could mean that **I have fear or ego issues.**

So, what do high-authorization leaders do with new ideas, innovations and problem-solving strategies that *really could* improve on the excellent work of associates?

First, we can always ask. "If you're open, I have some ideas that could help us accomplish our hopes. How do you feel about letting me make some suggestions?"

Some leaders read that paragraph and react, "Are you kidding? I'm the boss! Are you saying that I have to ask permission to lead?"

Permission isn't the right word. But in *asking* versus *telling*, we show true respect and build a sense of partnership. We're more likely to engender corresponding respect from the type of person we want in this model. That person, hopefully, isn't unteachable or closed to input, but also isn't used to taking orders.

So ask. I want associates who self-initiate and really move out. So it's an imposition to impose too much of myself. I think I'm helping but I'm actually laying down speed bumps.

For example, I've always operated as a self-initiating executive. Because I've been supervised by boards, I went decades without a real boss. But years ago, a board chairman began behaving as if he were my boss. His attitude wasn't condescending, but his approach required a whole new behavior: he gave me assignments and directives about how to do "my job." They weren't unfair or unreasonable or ill-conceived directives. He was a strong, bright, competent, thoughtful person.

So what's the problem? Simply this: my days and weeks were already jammed with strategies and tactics that fit my style and approach, and those actions were already producing positive effects. **His directives were piling on!**

What I wanted to ask was, "Which things *that I've been doing successfully for years* would you like me to stop doing in order to fulfill your assignments?"

We negotiated together and found what worked for us. We sat and talked. Understanding led to a shared ownership of change initiatives that felt more collegial.

But that brief season showed me how others feel when I impose too much on them. **The initial impact of imposition is confusion, over-work and mental fatigue.** Personally, I felt micromanaged. For some personality types (and I *like* this type!) micromanagement feels stunting, even crippling. For people who are already keen leaders and self-starters, heavy-handed leadership will steal their joy and make them feel as if they're carrying a backpack filled with rocks to work every day.

So start by asking, not telling.

Another way for high-authorization leaders to introduce ideas is to **create contexts for cross-pollination** in every division or program. In other words, I can plan gatherings where everyone is invited to speak into each other's departments. This *group-think* means that all ideas get a hearing in a setting where everyone expects to receive some candid suggestions.

Of course, some people will *hate* this. "What does that schmo know about what I'm doing?"

But overall, this raises the bar of excellence and gives high-performers confidence that other related divisions aren't in the hands of people who will affect the whole enterprise in negative ways.

Watch Out for Your Own Expertise

Another danger lurks. I might be prone to meddle in an area of my own considerable experience and expertise. Because my knowledge in that realm is high, and because previous exploits were successful, it's difficult to disentangle my past glories from my current role.

My greatest temptation, for example, is to *micromanage by improvement* in the area of planning and executing church worship services. Because I'm a competent musician and very experienced in planning worship experiences in three churches, it's easy for me to meddle.

When my last church hired a hugely successful worship pastor whose gifts in that area outshine my own, it became downright silly for me to meddle and micromanage. But because of my own history and interest, I had to fight the temptation to be a nuisance. Our worship pastor was patient and understanding and invited me into the idea stages so that I didn't impose myself at the wrong times and in the wrong ways. But still, I'm sure I was a pain.

Why did I micromanage?

First, because I had lingering curiosity and passion for that area, which simply had to be redirected. But second, I meddled because **he wasn't doing it the same way I would have done it.** Even though his results were extraordinary, his tactics were *his tactics.* Which means that I had to learn how to let go.

Which reminds me of a time when a board member was meddling in my work. After plenty of painful interactions, we finally realized—we both wanted the same thing, **but I wasn't doing it his way.** He liked the results but had a hard time disentangling himself from managing my tactics. He had some expertise and experiences that made it tough to stand back and let me lead. And our leadership styles differed greatly.

Are there areas where you are prone to meddle? Is this because of a lack of confidence in your associate? Does some past failure haunt you? Or are you having a hard time letting go of hands-on management because this is one of your hobby-horses, or even a field of genuine expertise?

Depending on the answer, you might need to make changes, either in your staff or in your personal practices.

Giving Away Real Authority

That's what really needs to be given away—true authority. "This is your baby. If you succeed, it's your victory. If you fail, it's *my* failure because I chose you and everything happened on my watch."

With authorization and protection like that, most strong leaders flourish. They love their work and feel highly valued and trusted. They feel like associates, instead of employees.

An associate is a fellow, a partner, a co-laborer who works *with* me. An employee is someone who works *for* me.
I'd rather have people working *with* me; people who want to succeed, not in order to please me, or out of fear of disappointing me, but because they share emotional ownership in the enterprise in the healthiest ways.

Even in a volunteer culture, authorization imparts freedom and a sense of value and respect. Sometimes volunteers fall short of my hopes. While I try to be gracious and patient, there are times when volunteers are simply serving in an area where they lack skill, time or general capacity for success. As long as their efforts are good-spirited, the organization barely suffers those deficits. If the volunteers feel supported even in the hard moments, they will likely be open to a new and different role that better suits their gifts and passions. Since the only paycheck a volunteer ever gets is a sense of satisfaction (from God's blessing and people's thanks), the spirit of respect and appreciation is more important in the long run than the actual product or service that is being provided.

A Formula That Works for Volunteers

Some organizations are mostly made up of volunteers. In these not-for-profit enterprises, the real commodity is spirit. With that in mind, the greatest mistake is thinking that good strategy will supersede a floundering spirit. In a volunteer organization, it simply won't. **If people aren't having a good time doing worthy things, they'll stop participating.** Even in for-profit companies, this is true. A good strategy might accomplish real gains and bolster good spirit. But if the spirit of the culture is bad, those gains will be short-lived.

So I use this table to remind executives and associates of the ways in which strategy and spirit combine to affect people. Then, I ask them to communicate these truths to those who manage their projects:

A good strategy plus a good spirit =   *+20*

A bad strategy plus a good spirit   = *+5*

A good strategy plus a bad spirit   = *-5*

A bad strategy plus a bad spirit   = *-20*

High-authorization cultures feed the good spirit that fuels high-level enthusiasm, commitment and performance. They also create community, which leads to sustainability. **People love to work, and keep working, in places where they feel freedom, respect and collegiality.** If I'm only a cog in a machine or a replaceable part in an impersonal operation, I'm likely to lose interest.

If there is a person who prefers to be only a functionary in a corporation that lacks community, that's not the person I'm looking to hire. I want people who are committed to people and I want people interested in producing a product or service that genuinely helps people.

If you're here to punch in, follow orders and collect a paycheck, you're not the associate that I'm looking for. I want leaders who actually care, and I want to authorize them to really make a difference. I want my colleagues to feel empowered and emboldened to maximize their skills and influence without fear of heavy-handed leadership from me. As Dennis Bakke writes, "When teams handle a variety of tasks, individuals are able to make full use of their skills, and work becomes more challenging and enjoyable....The primary factor in determining whether people experience joy or drudgery in the workplace is the degree to which they control their work."[41]

Pulling a Gorbachev

Are there moments when grabbing authority is necessary versus sharing authority?

Yes. One of the greatest leaders of the 20th century was Mikhail Gorbachev. For decades, much of the world suffered under the plague of communism. The people of the Soviet Union had endured generations of harsh rule and sad, gray reality. Gorbachev clearly sensed the need for more freedom and for a system like democracy that relies on the trusts, rights and responsibilities of a respectful, free society—where authority is shared.

At a critical time in history, the USSR was losing the Cold War and many Soviet people hoped to throw off the oppression of communism. In 1982, after the death of Leonid Brezhnev, the predictable succession of leaders would have placed a harsh over-lord in power to crush rising opposition and to tighten the reins of power, like Stalin, Khrushchev and Brezhnev had done. Yuri Andropov briefly succeeded Brezhnev, but died in 1984. Then, Mikhail Gorbachev rose to the highest office in the USSR with an agenda that proved itself over time. Clearly, it was Gorbachev's intent to redistribute authority into healthier hands and healthier systems.

In order to do that, **Gorbachev virtually grabbed king-like powers in the critical years of 1989-1991**. Critics on both sides (Soviet communists and nationalistic reformers) complained that Gorbachev was dangerously close to establishing a dictatorship. The Supreme Soviet granted him increasing levels of executive power.[42] Then, **when Gorbachev could have thrown his power around, he actually gave it away**. His notion of *glasnost* (openness) transitioned the Soviet government into a more

---

[41] Bakke, Dennis. *Joy at Work: A Revolutionary Approach to Fun on the Job.* Seattle: PVG, 2006.
[42] *www.Wikipedia.org*

democratic system. Walls came down. Countries enslaved by the Soviet empire were set free to establish their own governance. The Russians pursued peace with their previous enemies, like the USA. The world became a safer place.

While most politicians appear to have enormous egos, Gorbachev did not seem to love power. I don't know if he accomplished all he hoped, but I know I'm grateful he landed on the human scene in my lifetime. The world is better off because the person who made the power grab apparently did not crave power.

In Tolkien's great trilogy, *The Lord of the Rings*,[43] **the ring of power is only safe (and barely safe) in the hands of a hobbit;** a being predisposed toward humility and without a hunger for the power the ring could wield.

In the Bible's classic account of sin and redemption, the heroic work of rescuing the world could only be accomplished by a rescuer (Jesus) who did not regard his divine authority as "something to cling to…instead, he humbled himself."[44]

People who don't love power simply handle power more effectively.

Consolidation for Redistribution

In every organization, there are times for consolidating authority in order to redistribute it into healthier hands and healthier systems. This is the crux of catalyzing most turnarounds and reorganizations. Influence has to be wrestled carefully out of the hands of those who are not leading successfully, and then redistributed into the hands of a new cast of leaders.

---

[43] Tolkien, J. R. R. *The Lord of the Rings.* New York: Houghton-Mifflin, 1988.
[44] *Philippians* 2:6

Even then, there are ways to include associates, and even let them lead the way. One of my executive leadership teams decided to restructure with considerable influence from Patrick Lencioni's books.[45] Lencioni calls for new levels of community, trust and mutual accountability. Part of the beauty of our tough but worthy shift was that the impetus rose up like a groundswell from my associates. Under the force of their passion, I was challenged to adapt and adopt new ways of thinking and being.

Of course, I had the authority to shut down innovation at any time. But instead, I tried to embrace the changes, learned a ton and grew as a leader. And my colleagues felt empowered and energized in a renewed leadership culture.

The danger for leaders, again, is ego. Like Tolkien's terrible ring, **the longer and tighter we hold power, the more dangerous *it* and *we* become**. Power is almost always corrupting, and those who wield it well are those who spread it around generously. The best leaders, like Jesus, are somewhat hobbit-like in their purity— "shrewd as serpents, and as innocent as doves," said Jesus.[46] They simply don't need the power. They come to serve, not to be served. They share authority easily. Imagine the Son of God saying to a band of disciples, "All authority in heaven and earth has been given to me. Now go, make disciples, baptize and teach. I give the ongoing work to you."[47] He gave authority to them and left the redemption of the world in the hands of ordinary fishermen and tax collectors. Amazing.

---

[45] Lencioni, Patrick. *Death by Meeting: A Leadership Fable…About Solving the Most Painful Problem in Business.* San Francisco: Jossey-Bass, 2004.
[46] *Matthew* 10:16
[47] *Matthew* 8:28-29

Chapter Eight

Affirmation: You're a Valuable Asset

People thrive on affirmation. Affirmation fuels energetic, fully invested people more than money. The affirmation of respected peers is a huge incentive. Affirmation isn't everything, but it's a big part of what gets people up and keeps people going.

Coaches who don't know the power of honest affirmation are missing a catalytic element in motivating teams. Teachers who forget to affirm the positive will discourage the greater portion of their students. Leaders who neglect affirmation starve the organic growth and progress of the enterprises they're expending enormous energy to nurture.

It's hard to imagine why any perceptive leader would ignore this critical tool. Perhaps some leaders think, "I got to this place without a lot of backslapping. Why should I stroke other people's egos?" Or maybe verbal affirmation is embarrassing for us, so we assume that others would be embarrassed. Or withholding affirmation is about creating mystique and keeping others guessing regarding their standing in the organization. "If I affirm them, they might get self-important and relax too much."

Whatever the reason, when leaders don't affirm, we're robbing our organizations of fuel and force.

The Many Faces of Affirmation

Affirmation can be expressed in many ways. For some, **words are the best vehicle** for communicating respect and appreciation to valued associates. There are people with active verbal receptors—words carry a lot of weight. These types of people would rather work for lower pay in an environment of warm verbal interchange than for higher pay in a place that's too task-driven to spend time stroking each other. For those who put more value in words, there can even be an allergy to work cultures where relational nuances, like affirmation, are an afterthought.

For others, words are suspect and less important. **Tangible demonstrations of appreciation** are preferred. For some of these people, nothing speaks with as much force as money. Money is symbolic and loaded with meaning. Salaries, gifts and bonuses speak volumes about respect and standing in the company.

For still others, **social or strategic inclusion** carries a load of value. Dennis Bakke writes, "I believe refraining from forming friendship or taking time to know and love people does immense damage to the spirit of everyone in the workplace."[48] An invitation to a privileged gathering or a coveted event builds esteem. It communicates interest and breeds camaraderie.

Still, the simplest form of affirmation is the

---

[48] Bakke, Dennis. *Joy at Work: A Revolutionary Approach to Fun on the Job*. Seattle: PVG, 2006.

kind word of praise. "Your _____ [ideas, energy, optimism, talent?] brings a great contribution to what we're doing." Fill in the blank. Or even just say, "Thanks. I see all you're doing."

In volunteer organizations, the word of affirmation (any show of appreciation) is an emotional boost or bonus. Yes, there are other rewards to volunteering time, talent and treasure. We receive personal satisfaction, acquire new skills and enjoy professional and personal connections. Any noble effort can be its own reward. Still, **affirmation is the primary compensation that we have to offer.**

Few people work in order to be affirmed, but most benefit from it. Some don't *need* affirmation in order to flourish; but why should a leader run the risk of depriving them? Some *say* they don't need affirmation, or any show of appreciation; but when it doesn't come, they withdraw and aim their benevolence or loyalty in other directions.

Thin affirmation is counterproductive. Most people can sniff a counterfeit and despise flattery. So use restraint. An ancient proverb says, "If you find honey, eat just enough—too much of it and you will vomit."[49] If people feel schmoozed or glad-handed, they feel used. Affirmation should be honest, based on actual observations and genuine appreciation.

This means cultivating in our own lives an eye for what we appreciate in others. We have to take the time to pay attention, allow our own hearts to be affected by others and then deliver affirmation from an authentic place.

Again, It's Not All about Words

One long-time associate deflected all of my verbal affirmation and gently teased, "Remember, I have three children moving toward college." He preferred a raise or a

---

[49] *Proverbs* 25:16

bonus over a compliment.

Another associate reminded me that my verbal affirmations "can be like drinking from a fire hose." A few words aptly chosen might accomplish more than many compliments expressed often. "I'd rather have a frequent exchange of ideas and a stronger sense of real partnership," he told me.

A third associate, new to our circle, reminded me, "More quality time together would make me feel like a true part of the team and a fully constituted leader. Can we play some golf together?"

Still, even while I try to affirm everyone according to their receptors, I don't withhold the words. If I did, all of them would gradually feel undervalued or insecure—which breeds subtle discontent and stifles confidence, creativity and energy.

When There's Nothing Complimentary to Say

If I can't affirm someone often, or if I can't affirm someone genuinely, the wrong person is on the bus. It's time to build an exit strategy. That person will do better elsewhere and our enterprise will do better with a new face on the team.

When this person is a volunteer, displacement can be tricky business. We don't want to dismiss kindness too readily. And the entire volunteer culture can be impacted if one contributor is handled roughly.

Still, there are times for change. However painful, instigating staff change can be the most important work of the executive. We need the courage to confront and the wisdom to make changes when necessary, or else everyone will eventually be affected in other ways—through compromised service, products and potentials. Sometimes even the loss of the whole organization.

Keeping the Best People

In a high-authorization culture with highly competent, self-initiating associates, creative affirmation is often the key to enlisting and keeping the very best people. The best people are looking to develop and utilize their considerable gifts in a context where their contributions are well-leveraged and highly valued. The very best talent will often stay if they feel that their roles are not constantly subordinated. People who perceive they are granted real authority and honest appreciation are likely to pursue a longstanding relationship—even without enormous pay or the lure of promotion.

Not everyone should climb the ladder. One of my past superstar associates moved into a ten-year experiment as a CEO. Loyalty to the organization, strong appeals from the board and some personal curiosity drew him in. And possibly the pay raise. He had a big family and needed to be thinking of long-term financial hopes.

By my observation, he did very well in that top role—at least a nine on a scale of ten. But he later told me, "I was miserable. I was using secondary gifts and I actually shrunk the scope of my influence. I'm not cut out for that kind of work."

Many people assumed he could only be fulfilled and by stepping into a "higher role." But after leaving that position, superstar days are ahead of him again. He's an eleven-plus in a truer calling and excels like never before.

Not Everyone is Cut Out for Senior Leadership

In the American church, people are just now learning that some pastors aren't destined be *lead* pastors. They might have enormous gifts in care, teaching, program building and administration, with deficits in, or even distaste for, aspects of executive leadership.

For decades, well-meaning parishioners have chided, "When are you going to be a *real* pastor?" or, "When are you going to have your *own* church?" Under those pressures, many highly influential and truly successful associate pastors take a so-called "step up" into disastrous seasons of disappointment. Their roles no longer match their gifts. Only now, with the rise of thousands of multiple-staff churches, are American parishioners learning to *affirm* role-specific associates as fully ordained and vested pastors.

In other vocations, valuable associates are coaxed and teased (even by their spouses) to climb to the top, as if the top is the ultimate sphere of influence and privilege. As a young man, I was given the book, *See You at the Top,* by Zig Ziglar.[50] Nice gift, nice sentiment and a very helpful book about reaching personal potential. But what is "the top?" Am I sure I really want to get there?

Trina Paulus' book, *Hope for the Flowers,*[51] is a children's book with messages for every age. It's the story of a caterpillar who follows the crowd on a treacherous climb. When he reaches the top, he sees that the whole heap of squirming fuzz is nothing more than a "caterpillar pillar" on which the fuzzy creatures are climbing all over each other on the way to nowhere. In the end, he reaches the top and is thrown off the pile. He hits bottom, only to discover a better way to live and aspire. As you can imagine, he isn't a caterpillar forever.

In our world, some super-associates spiral downward from the fateful moment they succumb to the pressure to climb. New pressures come to bear; new talents and focus are required. It isn't a *better* role at all. It's just a different one.

---

[50] Ziglar, Zig. *See You at the Top.* Gretna, LA: Pelican Publishing, 1977.
[51] Paulus, Trina. *Hope for the Flowers.* Mahwah, NJ: Paulist Press, 1997.

The Truth About Executive Leaders

In truth, **some of the best future executive leaders are less effective associates and managers**. Why? They see the big picture and struggle with details. Program management requires an eye for detail and a habit of micro-control that is counterproductive and counterintuitive for top leaders. The best executive leaders see the big picture and enlist and support (authorize) others to manage the details. Sometimes strong administrative help allows those managers to use executive style leadership to accomplish management objectives, but it's still not always a great fit.

For corresponding reasons, **detailed manager-types tend to fail in executive roles**—I'll call it Jimmy Carter syndrome. With the right kind of affirmation (authentic and expressed in a manner that fits the makeup of the recipient), the best managers will feel authorized to stay in critical management roles. With the right kind of affirmation, the best associates will have the courage to remain in their associate roles, maintaining and growing their considerable influence without the need to jump ship to other places where they are appreciated—or enticed to leap out of their best skill set and into a role for which they aren't equipped. How many great assistant coaches have failed as head coaches, simply because the roles require different skill sets.

When We See a Leader of Leaders

When I see big-picture people in the organization who are obviously geared to be top-level leaders, I want to affirm them, help them grow and unleash them. They'll either become my successors or launch new initiatives—ideally as part of our work. Wherever they go, they can no longer be contained or restrained.

Sometimes, this is my contribution to the broader good—launching a great leader. How many great coaches came up under John Wooden, Bill Walsh and other coaching legends and were *set free* to do their thing elsewhere?

So I want to give them my keen interest and generous portion of affirmation and encouragement. If people don't feel valuable, they will under-perform, compromise the effectiveness of the enterprise or move elsewhere. If they do feel valued, the best people flourish and stay.

Chapter Nine

Accountability: *Your Wellness Matters*

In any high-authorization culture, our greatest risk is the failure of trusted associates. What if associates don't handle freedom and empowerment well? What if I "get rid of the ball quickly and put it in the hands of people who can make plays,"[52] but they fumble or drop the pass?

With potential fumbles and drops in mind, our associates need accountability. People need to be held to a high standard and encouraged to perform at high levels. Excellence matters and performance affects the product or service we're trying to provide.

Still, many of us displace our keenest oversight and accountability. We tend to watch out for programmatic failure, when **the real risk is personal failure**. We see the slide in quality and production, but miss human spirals that underlie the diminishing outcomes.

---

[52] Craig, Roger, Bill Walsh and Matt Maiocco. *Tales from the San Francisco 49ers Sideline.* Champaign: Sports Publishing L.L.C., 2004.

Healthy People Do Healthy Things

In general, healthy people do good work in sustainable ways.

Occasionally, healthy people do poor work. Healthy people can be incompetent or ill-prepared for a role.

Sometimes, unhealthy people do good work in spurts and sputters. For some unhealthy people, work life can be the one place of sanity and success.

But as a rule, healthy people produce quality products and services. If healthy people can't produce healthy products and services, then those healthy people are probably playing out of position. To borrow again from Collins, they might be "the right people on the bus, but in the wrong seats."[53]

Assuming we have the right people on the bus, and assuming they're in the right seats, they should know their parts of the business **better than I do**. As long as they stay healthy, they will produce quality outshining anything I could conjure. In other words, I'm going to find associates who can, when they're healthy, do their parts of our business better than me. That's the heart of high-authorization leadership.

Displaced Accountability

If I can find and empower excellent people, then heavy programmatic accountability (micro-management) will be viewed as amateurish meddling. How well I've learned to read the patronizing smile of trusted associates telling me, "Thanks for the input, boss, but I've got this one."

I have a choice. I can either resent their hints that I'm in over my head or I can celebrate having people that

---

[53] Jim Collins, *Good to Great.* New York: HarperCollins, 2001.

go deeper in their specific fields than I could possibly go. The payoff for the organization is widespread competence in a context of mutual respect. The payoff for me is the freedom to apply my energies elsewhere and to rest in the competence of others. It's good to trust great people!

So my relative ignorance is no slight against me. I have other broad-level matters that demand executive leadership (inculcating values, fostering cohesion, imparting vision, launching new initiatives). **My relative ignorance is not only normal—it's optimal.** When I have more knowledge about a particular aspect of the enterprise, (or when I *think* I do), the temptation is to meddle, which is, ultimately, an act of disrespect. The best associates will broil and burn under the impositions of micromanagement; or else they'll craft strategies to patronize the boss while doing their own thing.

Holding a Person Accountable for Health

Better than programmatic accountability, what the best people really need is *personal* accountability. *Are you healthy? How's your family? What are you doing for exercise? What kinds of experiences inspire you? Are you growing as a person? What are you reading these days?*

We can ask those questions in group-share settings at staff meetings and breakaways. We can do walk-arounds, affirming and greeting anyone and everyone any day of the week, building relationships that foster trust and openness. Most important, we can be transparent about our own wellness, inviting honesty and risk. With trust, openness and honesty, genuine personal accountability can find form.

In many organizations, the low point on the wall is left unguarded—**personal, moral, ethical, spiritual, emotional health.** The breakdown and fall of key people puts the whole organization at risk.

When a program fails, we just fix it, or improve it, or dump it. It hurts, but so what?
When *people* fail, real harm is done. Wounded people wound other people. Wounded people do bad work. Wounded people hurt the organization. Hurting people have more difficulty focusing, producing and committing. When people implode, everyone suffers.

Depression alone costs the American marketplace tens of billions—possibly hundreds of billions—of dollars annually in worker productivity. **Divorce** wreaks the same kind of havoc. **Addictions** bring astronomical costs and losses. Even simple **fatigue** can be calamitous.

People who are spiraling in their personal lives are less likely to dream with clarity, strategize rationally or work diligently. Products and services suffer and the collective culture of the organization walks with a limp. To borrow from the Apostle Paul, "When one part of the body suffers, every part suffers with it."[54] Not irredeemably, but for a season. The long or short of that season depends, of course, on leadership.

Realize, the occasional wounded genius can blow onto the scene and change the landscape with brilliant innovation, and then blow away. In one of my stops, we took a risk and hired with full knowledge a huge talent whose personal life was in need of reconstruction. At the end of his short tenure, aspects of his private life came to pieces. But those several months were fantastic. He opened our eyes, raised our standards, enlisted talented people and left a legacy that served us for years.

All the while, my accountability wasn't focused on his program or division. He knew that arena far better than I did. I cozied up really close and tried to nurture his soul and prolong our privileged season. I wanted him to heal

---

[54] 1*Corinthians* 12:26

and grow and find a future with dignity. And if things didn't work in sustainable ways, I wanted to be in position to contain the damage and carry our success forward.

That's essentially what happened. I could not fix his life, but I believe I helped him stay relatively healthy through crisis. And through it all, he made a huge positive impact.

In another setting, an associate suffered a family hardship. While the details were known by only a few, we were able to provide counseling throughout the ordeal. We built a stronger team around the affected leader so his sadness and stress didn't undo the gains that he'd painstakingly catalyzed through the years. We enlisted other leaders to secure a landing strip of health, grace and usefulness once the crisis was over. A situation that could have brought real unrest to the organization ended up being a season of growth and understanding. The entire enterprise learned lessons about community, care and the power of grace. Flowers grew out of the mulch of emotional loss. In my opinion, it was our greatest season.

CEO as Shepherd

I know that not all organizational leaders are pastors. But the word *pastor* means *shepherd.* **Every executive leader is a shepherd.** Sometimes a shepherd stands on a high hill, scanning the horizon for fertile fields. Other times, we're walking among the flock, inspiring, listening and nurturing. But we're all shepherds.

If we can't do the nurturing part, then a nurturer ought to be our very first hire. If we lack the relational skills to tend to the flock, then we'd better find a close associate who can do it for us—otherwise the people and the work environment will deteriorate.

And if I can't find that nurturing presence?

Well, *just do find it.* Make it a priority as high as finding the best technicians, managers and innovators. If I can't or won't make that effort, I'm going to either wear myself out trying to be what I'm not or the welfare of my fellows will suffer; and all of us will suffer the outcomes.

I have a friend and mentor who went to a huge enterprise and said, "I can save you millions of dollars a year in lost productivity and employee turnover simply by teaching communication skills throughout the organization." The company took the dare and ended up paying my friend for his shepherding work—a very humble amount, by the way, in light of the millions of dollars saved. In essence, he nurtured workers, taught healthy communication and helped everyone bring their "A games" to the effort.

The Full Court Press

Some robust enterprises succeed by burning out and burning through people. These high-demand cultures with heavy hierarchies and even heavier expectations can be successful, usually in the short term. If the monetary rewards are lavish enough, people will endure great hardships to be part of a company like this. Some people even live for that kind of pressure!

Most people, however, eventually quit. And the organization turns into a punch-line for a whole slough of jokes.

At the high school or college level of basketball, there are teams that occasionally succeed by applying a full-court-press through the entire game. Rick Pitino is a college coach who brings this hardcore, frenetic approach to every team he coaches. He's had success.

But this strategy only works when the team has great quickness and enough depth to substitute freely. Without depth, and plenty of rest for the weary, the non-stop full-court press is a recipe for failure, injury and burnout.

At the pro basketball level, non-stop full-court press is a free pass to an early fishing season. The pros know how to break the press. They've learned to keep their composure. They've learned the art of spacing and pacing with focused outbursts of energy.

Novices who watch professional basketball will be prone to say, "They don't look like they're working that hard. I'll bet a good college team could beat these guys."

The truth? No, the collegians can't beat the pros. The pros are the elite of the sport and they've learned how *not* to waste energy; rather, how to focus energy where it matters most.

While I'm no fan of the poor shooting and ball movement that characterize today's NBA, I do know this— winning requires a unique combination of morale, unity, health and a clear differentiation of roles. The best coaches care about the whole person. Trainers are more important than any of us will ever know. Team chaplains and sports psychologists offer their good help. And the overall health of off-the-court relationships with spouses and between players affect the mix with private dramas that virtually guarantee public outcomes.

Greg Jamison, a seasoned and successful executive in the world of professional sports management, told me, "Winning isn't only about what happens on the ice. At the end of the day, teams win because of a whole subtext of relationships and chemistry and health issues. Everything has to come together."

The Business of People

Whatever our professional environments, health and contentment lead to greater sustained productivity. Pacing and spacing issues matter. Relationships inside and outside the workplace greatly affect quality, productivity and sustainability. **If we think our associates' health and relational issues are none of our business, we really don't understand the business.**

- Healthy, energetic, rested and focused people do great work.

- Unhealthy, tired, distracted people wear down and drag others down.

- Healthy people lubricate the work environment.

- Unhealthy people grind away at the gears until the entire mechanism breaks down.

With that in mind, I'd almost always hire a healthier person with lesser talent before I'd hire a talented person with obvious issues. Of course, ideally, I'm going to hold out for the more-talented person with greater health.

But realize, **even the healthiest people have seasons that require special help and attention.** This is one worthy place to apply my energy. A simple "How are you?" coupled with ten minutes of active listening might affect outcomes more than a host of programmatic tweaks and thrusts. In other words, investing in the person is more likely to result in real gains. **Ignoring the person while adjusting the program can be like giving a fresh trail map to a hiker with a broken leg.**

Even more, building a culture of healthy relationships, healthy pacing and healthy habits will cultivate sustainability and protect against catastrophic breakdown.

Many people have contributed to my own health and sustainability. One coach, for example, used to say, "Be quick but don't hurry," a statement that some people trace back to John Wooden. I apply that principle to everything. I'm capable of working in quick bursts of focused activity, but choose not to hurry in a way that increases the likelihood of mistakes and burnout. And I don't ever want to project at work or at home a frenetic, manic craziness that makes me unapproachable and impossible to live with. **I want to look like a picture of health because *I am actually healthy*.** This approach is contagious; it sets the tone of a home or work environment.

Here are some *specific, tactical encouragements:*

- **Get to work.** *None of this is an invitation to piddle around. Hard work is good for us and good for others.*

- **Pay attention to pacing.** *We are more likely to be engaged in a marathon than in a sprint. Some moments or seasons require more speed or energy, but no one can sprint an entire marathon.*

- **Project composure from authentic health.** *I'm not suggesting that we pose or project Falsehood. Find both personal contentment and healthy discontent with the product. Drive yourself and others to better your product with motivations better than fear and desperation. Excellence is a great motivation. So is genuine service to the community or the customer.*

- **Guard your own health.** *If you aren't healthy everyone will be affected. Get the spiritual, emotional, mental and physical helps and habits in place to sustain a healthy life. One* proverb says, *"Above all else, guard your heart, for it is the wellspring of life."*[55]

- **Promote the health of others**. *Ask. Facilitate. Resource. Prove that you actually care.*

- **Get rest**. *We all need sleep. Everyone benefits from time away, and especially those of us who think we don't need it. Learn the art of Sabbath-keeping and even sabbatical rest.*

- **Give rest**. *Establish a culture that honors rest in concert with hard work and excellence.*

- **Gear up for a long race**. *Again, remember pacing issues and be attentive to signs of corporate fatigue, as well as personal fatigue. Cultures can only tolerate innovations and blitzes in periodic or metered ways, or else they become frazzled and disjointed. Know your culture and its capacities.*

- **Watch out for casualties** *strewn along the road. You won't always be able to help, but often you can.*

- **Race to win.**

In any high-authorization culture, our greatest risk is the failure of trusted associates. **While programmatic failure sets us back,** *people who come undone* **deal a blow to the organization that is truly dire.** Their programs suffer and their work environments suffer; the

---

[55] *Proverbs* 4:23

organization suffers. Then, if recovery is impossible, we end up cycling through the hiring process again and again while expending huge energy and resources orienting new talent.

How much better to invest in health. That's where the best accountability gets applied.

Whitewashing the Fence

Chapter Ten

Information: *What People Really Need to Know*

It looked like a match made in heaven. "Aging church seeks energetic, proven pastor to turn the inward focus outward, reach more young families, revitalize worship and foster renewal." Since I'd seen similar results in previous settings, my wife and I considered pulling our family away from an established situation to venture out and answer this call.

As we considered this move, the church hummed quietly with encouraging vital signs and showed promise of greater things. The departing pastor shared many of my philosophical bents and clearly made gains in plowing the field for innovation. The people were thoughtful and committed; the search committee was winsome. Their hopes and visions lined up beautifully with mine.

But the buildings were stiff and archaic. The language of the written materials painted word pictures that reminded me of the church of my childhood—thirty years ago. "A good time was had by all."

The programs and structures felt heavy, with policy and process getting more play than innovation and accomplishment. All in all, the organization had the feel of an old Chevy Impala—nice to look at, with some rumbling power under the hood, but tough to handle.

Meeting with the Board in the second round of interviews, I asked, "Do you intend to be an island of static change-resistance in the middle of the most dynamic change culture [Silicon Valley] in the world?"

The awkward silence gave way to one of the older members, whose voice clearly held some sway. "We know that we've been an island. But we also know that we need to learn how to do things in a new way."

I believed him then and I believe him now. He spoke for many of the leaders.

Though not all.

I soon learned that some strong people would dig in their heels, protect their turf and cling to power. While I'd seen some of this in two previous jobs, I was astonished how vigorous a few people were. While the church at large responded marvelously and the greater portion of the leaders proved engaging and flexible, a few people made the first year almost unbearable. For the first time in my career I wondered if I would have to leave a job undone— for the sake of my health, my family and the unity of the organization.

Then it all opened up. Thankfully and wonderfully, things got better.

The Old Bait and Switch

Reflecting on the journey from interested outsider to executive candidate to newly installed leader, the phrase, "bait and switch" kept coming to my lips. I was handed reams and piles and notebooks of information, but people were too polite to give me a short list of critical information pieces I needed. "This is what you will *really* face if you come here." No one showed me a map of the sophisticated minefield of subtle obtrusions, made explosive by the long history and stubborn attitudes in a few sub-cultures.

In part, they withheld because of the culture of *niceness* that permeates many organizations—"I didn't want to say anything mean about anyone else."

In part, they spared me good information because of a serious lack of time in the mirror. In fact, after hiring a consultant to give them some mirror-time, they fired the consultant. They didn't like what he saw in their mirror.

It's possible that with the full truth I would never have taken the job. So in a twisted way, after years of satisfying work, I'm grateful. Still...even the strongest self-initiating leaders need good information. **If I'm going to authorize those leaders fully, I also need to inform them completely in order to avoid the bait and switch.**

What kind of information do highly competent people need in order to do the job we're asking them to do?

A Map of the Minefields

First, authorized leaders **need to really know what they're up against.** While no one can anticipate every booby-trap or identify every giant in the land, we want to reduce the bait-and-switch potential as much as humanly possible. People need to know the size and nature of the mountain they're about to climb. No one likes buyer's remorse, especially newly hired leaders.

This might even involve some transparency about **the hurdles that working with *me* will present.** "Here are the things that have frustrated people in the past...here are the ways I am likely to disappoint you...." Over-promising is a terrible habit that always leads to under-delivering. I want people to know what I *can* do for them and I need to help them prepare for what I *can't* deliver.

But mostly, *the minefield map* means helping people understand the terrain, with red flags strategically positioned to help associates brace for resistance and interference.

Years ago, I sat down with a new volunteer leader in a critical area of an organization. As I told him where the mines were buried, I'm sure I made him a bit nervous. But it seemed better that he should know what to expect. I spelled out just what he'd be up against and what he'd have to overcome if he hoped to leave that program in a better place than where he found it. I told him what I *did* have to offer and what I couldn't or wouldn't provide. He went away with a clearer picture of the task ahead of him and the authorization to complete it. He made some real gains.

The Bigger Picture

Second, authorized leaders need to **know how their valued influence fits into a bigger picture.** The most successful divisions can actually harm the whole if people don't understand how the larger body of work fits together. **Wonderful mavericks can overstep and outpace others in ways that throw the symmetry of an organization out of whack.** Like a fourteen-year-old whose frame outgrows his coordination, **growth without connectivity breeds clumsiness.**

Good information about connectivity is critical. "This is how your part **fits** in the whole... This is how **others** are helping you and how your success can feed others... This is where we're all going... This is the **plan**... This is the **optimum pace of change** and growth... This is the **vision** of where we'll be in five years. Shape your vision into the whole vision, building your arm to fit into the larger body."

Core Values

Third, authorized leaders **need to know the core values that drive the entire organization.** Without an understanding of those driving values and the deeply-held convictions owned by key fellows, highly authorized leaders will shred protocol, slay sacred cows and otherwise wreak havoc. Without respect for core values, those highly authorized leaders will be viewed as troublemakers and outsiders. Their change initiatives, no matter how well-intentioned and well-conceived, will suffer obstinate resistance from others.

In a previous stint, we hired a pastor of youth ministries. After a nationwide search, we pulled off a coup—we found an experienced, talented leader from a successful program. He was a self-initiating, marvelously focused pastor who was destined to transform our youth culture, where we'd suffered setbacks.

I started informing him of some deeply held values that he would need to embrace in order to succeed. Some of those values predated us both. Some were born of my initiation. For example, we valued being an intergenerational church, especially because the church was situated in a retirement community. So any sweeping changes on behalf of younger people needed to find their place in concert with older people, with a respectful view of traditional modes. All in all, he would have freedom to build something with his own signature, but he'd be a co-signer—this congregation (and their senior pastor) also had some deeply-rooted convictions.

He proved to be **very adept at contextualizing his vision.** He taught the teens to value and respect the seniors. Teens showed up *en masse* to sing traditional hymns, actually leading and serving at experiences that other teens might have considered boring or passé. And the seniors adored the teens and gave them emotional freedom and financial resources to innovate and infuse the church with youthful energy.

That one hire transformed the entire culture. We learned together how to navigate a complex field of passionately held traditions while still bringing innovation.

About Sacred Cows

Some sacred cows, of course, need to be slain. Some deeply held convictions are terribly flawed. **By clinging desperately to obsolete ways of thinking or behaving, we counter our own best wishes and sabotage our highest goals**. Sometimes it takes new people with new eyes to help us see how silly it is to honor practices that aren't worthy of such reverence.

But even then, the bloodletting has to be done carefully. If I'm asking associates to do the hard work of bringing innovation where the common viewpoint is emotionally entrenched, I need to be prepared to protect them vigorously against the backlash. In fact, I need to get out ahead of the change, like a pulling guard in football gets out ahead of a tailback on an end sweep. I don't want my fast, new star to be exposed to injury. And I want success.

But assuming that most of our driving values can hold up under scrutiny—in other words, they *aren't* sacred cows at all — we must be sure that our associates know those values and share them.

A Sad Story

It's always painful to have to let a talented person

go elsewhere. But in one case, it became absolutely necessary.

And oh, he was talented. His program grew. His constituents loved him.

But in our culture, we valued teamwork and mutual respect. He was a lone wolf. He built a small team of leaders who were loyal to him more than to the organization. He showed up late for staff meetings and offered a nominal—even hostile—presence. He pushed up against his supervisor incessantly, requiring constant accountability and several interventions of every kind.

We were building a culture based on some non-negotiable elements. One player simply wasn't playing according to our game plan. In truth, he infected others with similar discontent and made the staff culture—which had been a decidedly positive one—suffer the scrutiny of others in ways that affected us for years, even after his departure.

By the way, the people most likely to offend core values are the ones most likely to evidence weariness about the steady drumbeat of repetition regarding core values. **The ones who dread staff meetings where core values are recapitulated tend to be the most likely ones to build insular programs that fail to be integrated into the whole.**

Even against complaints, **critical core values need perpetual repetition**. People are forgetful. All of us develop bad habits. Whether we hang posters on the wall or invent litanies or chants or songs to reinforce our values, they can't be ignored or offended. **If our programs are the *boats we float*, core values are the *waves and tides and currents that float those boats*.**

I phrase core values in slogans for the sake of memory:

- *Healthy people do healthy work.* So let's care for the personal and spiritual welfare of others.

- *People over programs.* Programs are vehicles that bring people together for worthy purposes. But it's really about the people.

- *Spirit over strategy.* The right things done in the wrong spirit will disappoint terribly.

- *A culture that says "yes."* If someone has a vision or a dream, that person and idea will have a hearing. We want to say "yes" and come alongside your best impulses toward innovation.

- *We're in this together.* Everyone matters. We can do more as a team than as individuals.

- *We're a grace-place.* Mistakes often mean that we're living on the edge of crucial risk, adventure and innovation. **If you're going to fall, fall forward.**

- *This is a high-authorization culture.* We want to empower you to give real leadership.

Some of these phrases become familiar to the entire organization. Some are familiar to specific circles of influence and leadership. A few are familiar only to top-level staff. But all of them are repeated to the point of rolling eyes and laughing groans. I want to communicate with so much repetition that people can finish sentences for me and lampoon me at my going away party.

Young and Old Organizations

In start-up enterprises, crucial values can be seeded into the DNA of the organization. Hit on the values early and often. This breeds streamlined homogeneity—a keen and clear sense of shared purpose right from the start.

In longstanding institutions, crucial values need to be reintroduced and recapitulated in stubborn and optimistic terms. Otherwise, **sentimental notions from an irretrievable past will entrench the organization in swampy change-resistance.** During transitional times, long-timers will scamper to fill power voids and to re-infuse the organization with values or behaviors that represent "the glorious days of old." **It's very hard to convince people that the past will never be the future.** There might be some parts and pieces of the past that can be dusted off and honored, but idolizing the past is always an exercise in walking backwards.

As we go forward, diversity in the realm of "how" (How do we pull this off? How does our team function?) is healthy and invigorating. Different people will develop diverse strategies and use tactics that fit their own personalities and approaches. But diversity in the realm of "what" (What are we here for? What are we *about*?) or the "who" (just who are we?) foster confusion, which breeds conflict and bottlenecks.

Don't Miss First Base

It's critical to identify and agree upon core values. It's critical to hire and enlist with core values in mind. *Will this person uphold and represent those values?*

Over the years, I've helped organizations progress from core **values** to **visions** to **objectives** to **strategies** to tactical action **plans**. Each leadership culture is unique, with diverse personalities and angles of approach to their goals. The content of my coaching has evolved in different seasons under various influences. But the truth remains unchanged—**if the core values aren't understood and embraced, it's like *missing first base*.** Even long-ball hitters will be *called out* if they miss first base.

Pete Rose, the Major League's all-time hits leader, didn't understand one of baseball's core values: betting on the game compromises the integrity of the competition.

Other embattled baseball stars cheated with performance-enhancing drugs that tainted every accomplishment in a game where the numbers of different generations are weighed against each other. Hank Aaron will forever be the emotional Home Run King because of the perception that his numbers aren't skewed by chemicals. The others, however talented, appear to have missed first base.

All of this is **doubly true in volunteer organizations**. Each new cast of players must be coached on driving values or else trouble comes at the implementation level—every level, really.

Part of that risk comes because volunteer organizations tend to enlist any willing soul who will say "yes," but might not embrace the core values that drive visions and strategies. No matter how well-intentioned, those willing souls will create drag, and even barriers, to the progress of the whole. It's nice when people say "yes", but they still have to be vetted and coached. For example:

- A Little League baseball coach teaches excellent fundamentals and wins games, but yells too often at the kids, or excludes less-talented players from participation. The coach missed first base.

- A youth worker teaches Bible lessons on Sunday, but models a crass lifestyle away from church. The youth worker missed first base.

These breeches in "code" yield one-step-forward, two-steps-backward outcomes. People need to know the code and own those *givens*. Building up young people and encouraging participation is more important than winning games. Personal integrity teaches more than Bible memorization. It seems obvious to most people, but deep values must be repeated over and over—and honored.

How we inculcate core values in the culture of an organization can be as diverse as our styles and personalities. The imperative of doing this, however, is universal. Some principles and values never change. Teach them over and over *ad-nausea.*

So:

1. Give a map of the **minefields.**

2. Paint the **bigger picture** and make sure everyone knows where he/she **fits.**

3. **Reinforce core values** over and over again.

Those morsels of information will feed your people for the long road to success.

Whitewashing the Fence

Chapter Eleven

Ideas: Mostly Upon Request

While I don't want to meddle in my associate's programs, I still have some good ideas and useful experiences. My associates might even ask for my input.

But it's counterproductive to impose too much input; sometimes even to suggest it. One of the greatest obstacles to progress is idea glut. Hearty, aggressive associates simply try to do too many things and try to honor too many agendas, sometimes out of respect for their supervisors.

Realize, I'm a big fan of gathering ideas from every direction. Think-tanks are a good thing, and why not invite even the janitor to jump in with ideas on how to improve our products and services. It's great when others have a crystal-clear set of ideas and an undiluted resolve to bring them into reality.

But an idea dump, especially from a *really helpful boss*, can dilute that resolve.

David, Goliath and Saul

In the Bible, a giant man named Goliath is threatening the armies of King Saul. One brave young man steps forward to fight the giant. Young David, a shepherd, intends to fight the giant by faith using a slingshot and a prayer.

Before he goes into battle, King Saul outfits David with Saul's own armor and sword. It's a thoughtful gesture. His significant armor has protected Saul in many battles. His trusty sword has slain other enemies. Saul doesn't want David to lose, suffer or to be vulnerable to the giant's size and weaponry.

But realizing how clunky and ill-fitting the armor is, David casts it off. He has to fight this battle in his own way with his own set of talents and vulnerabilities.

The end of the story is legendary—the baseline Cinderella story. David conquers Goliath.

One of the greatest marks of a leader is restraint. No area requires restraint like the realm of ideas. Because our own "armor and weapons" have served us well, we assume they will serve others equally well. Sometimes, they will. Other times, they won't. Regardless, a leader must be cautious about forcing associates to wear "*Saul's armor*."

A Standing Offer

Not that there shouldn't be a standing offer: "If you need ideas, come to me. I always have a few tucked away in my feeble brain." Most smart associates will take advantage of this offer, at least to compare their own ideas or to make sure strategies fit into the larger vision.

But I have to offer ideas in freehanded ways, with respect for my associates' expertise and experience. I need to remember the first A—authorization. This isn't *my baby*.

Responsible To, Not For

"Wait? Am I not ultimately responsible for this baby?" many senior executives initially react. The answer found in the best organizations is, "No, I'm responsible *to* it, not *for* it. And this is the part I play and the gift I give to the whole—high-authorization leadership."

This kind of leadership leads to:

- Mutual respect: A sense of worth permeating the leadership culture.

- Optimism: A can-do attitude that lifts the entire organization.

- Sustainability: An eagerness among associates to be loyal and stay engaged.

That notion of "responsible to, not responsible for" also allows us to sleep at night, since we don't carry the faulty sense that the weight of the whole organization rests "on my shoulders." This is a shared work with shared authority and shared responsibility. Not even the "whole baby" is "my baby." We're all in this together. We have each other. We all "own" the success or failure of the enterprise.

Send Before You Speak

Some associates do suffer observable dry spells. Ideas obviously aren't flowing.

The best way to shake and break those spells is to *send* people to experiences where they can swim in inspiring pools of ideas and strategies. Conferences and seminars and even graduate schools are awash with stimulation. Smart organizations budget and invest toward continuing education experiences that inspire and motivate. Short-sighted organizations starve their leaders of inspiration by being skimpy on helpful exposures.

Though I will add this: some people are "continuing education junkies" who have poor implementation skills. Those types are better off spending more time, energy and resources implementing a few good ideas, and spending less on gathering a bag of new tricks.

New Frontiers and Personal Whims

"So where do *my* ideas find expression?" asks the top executive. Sometimes ideas find a hearing in the think tank, where the whole staff gathers for dynamic interchange. But even there, the CEO can be the *big gorilla in the room* if he or she is too vocal. Others will clam up. Not good. I've made that mistake too many times.

Most of my ideas are expressed in the big-picture realm, and often on new frontiers where no one else has been authorized (yet). This is the beauty of having competent self-initiating associates—I can pour myself into compelling big issues and new frontiers while I entrust others with their areas of influence.

Most top-level executives live in the realm of big and new. Like Tom Sawyer, the next adventure is always calling. We are often better catalysts than sustainers. We do well to fix more of our gaze on larger currents and next big steps and let others sustain worthy ventures.

Or, in some cases, the freedom born from refusing to meddle allows us to hold on to a particular, smaller facet of the work that still delights us. From what I've heard, Walt Disney never let go altogether of the creative side of cartooning. Even though he exercised a very loose, high-authorization oversight of the Disney empire—his brother was the heartier managing executive—Walt still loved the art of cartooning. His freehanded approach to executive leadership in other realms allowed him to stay fresh in his area of passion.

Even then, I assume that Walt was a genius among many geniuses and not heavy-handed with his ideas. If he was heavy-handed, that part of the Disney legend did not survive to my knowledge.

Humility and Respect

All in all, this high-authorization model takes humility. If I view myself as the primary resident genius—and I've made this mistake before—others will feel disempowered and disrespected. More than that, the collective enterprise will be systematically **stunted by the limited scope of one person's genius.**

But what about George Steinbrenner, the New York Yankees' long-time owner? He and they have won a bunch of World Series! What about the field marshals and perfectionists—the intimidators—who have achieved great results with more controlling approaches?

There are times and places where that style appears successful, for whatever reason. But most leaders with a heavy, top-down approach will chase away other strong people. Look how many managers Steinbrenner plowed through! And look how much money they have, in a rich New York market, to buy tremendous players.

Meddlers also tend to stunt the emerging genius of up-and-comers. Part of the art of high-authorization leadership involves identifying up-and-comers and stoking the fire. We learn the difference between real genius and mere eccentricity; between someone with untapped potentials versus the person with remarkable capacities to disappoint. If true genius comes with eccentricity, then we learn to gauge how much eccentricity the organization can endure, absorb or manage without residual negative effect.

Really, though, genius isn't always necessary. What we need is an environment where everyone has a hearing. That culture will likely entice the best people to join in and stay in.

The classic micromanager has a hard time hearing the ideas of others. Preferring yes-people, the low-authorization leader loves those who take orders and follow directions. This classic middle-to-lower management behavior guarantees the limited scope of the enterprise and leads to a huge investment into hiring, rehiring and all the training that goes with each.

Most of Us Need Real Help

Of course, most of us need detail-oriented administrative assistants and associates—people who hold the particulars together. The best administrators in my sphere have been those who:

- **find a workable balance** between creative self-initiation and doing exactly what I ask them to do.

- **hear exactly what I need** and build strategies that are unique to their skill sets.

- are **highly intuitive** and anticipate problems.

- are **utterly honest and yet totally uncritical** about my weaknesses. They understand clearly that if my deficits did not exist, their positions would be unnecessary.

- in short, **make me look good,** while I try to help them find great satisfaction in their contributions.

I try to give administrators the honor they deserve and very clear directives to make their tasks and priorities as clean and clear as possible.

But for other associates, **I try to spare them my ideas and directives so I don't gum up the works.**

If they have no ideas, I have the wrong people.

If I don't trust their ideas, I have the wrong people.

If I can't find the right people, the problem is me.

Chapter Twelve

Intervention: I'm Here to Help

One summer, my associates had an idea and I affirmed and co-owned it. We wanted to transform the church courtyard into a video café where visitors with limited church experience could sit outside, sip coffee, watch the worship service on television and listen to the message in a safe place. This idea has gotten traction elsewhere, so we set out on an experimental adventure.

Then we went public with our intentions.

We didn't venture far. We hadn't counted the cost. This innovation involved dismantling an outdoor courtyard worship service during the summer that had enormous sentimental value. People—nice people—began to clamor against our idea. We even discovered that the resistance was multi-generational. Many seniors had actually started the courtyard service thirty years previous; and many teenagers felt more comfortable and engaged in *that* service than in any other. We were stomping on sacred turf! This was more of a *sacred horse* than a *sacred cow*. That courtyard service, for reasons proven over many years, was a crucial vehicle for building our community.

Some wise leaders on our Board intervened. Even though their usual habit was to authorize the staff and to protect us in our innovations, in this case they stepped in. In the clearest, most respectful terms, they urged us to rethink our innovative strategy.

They were right. It took humility to publicly admit that we'd been impetuous. But it also earned us some credibility within the church. "The leaders are listening to us."

So sometimes things go badly. Sometimes people entrusted with real authority and freedom miss the mark. Ideas fail. Strategies flop and thud. Programs languish.

It's Time for an Intervention

Some associates might need one intervention in an entire career. Like clockwork, they produce quality work and need very few rescues.

Others might need frequent interventions and yet, somehow, are worth the investment.

Usually, **frequent intervention means trouble—** someone is playing out of position or ignoring core values. This is probably the wrong person.

Still, all of us have failures. All of us have seasons when we're overrun by bad breaks, or we're uninspired for a host of reasons. All of us have tried something that just didn't work. All of us will need an intervention sometime. Sooner or later we'll need someone who cares enough— about the enterprise and us as individuals—to intervene so that struggle doesn't turn into failure.

Health as a First Priority

My first priority is the health of my associate. I'll intervene in a failing *life* as often as a failing program. The most devastating failures are personal, spiritual, emotional, ethical and moral. The most important question for me to ask a floundering associate is, "How are you?" If we have a relationship, the floodgates usually open. If not, I watch stonewalling behavior, or the associate wonders how safe I am and how honest to be with me.

Again, my assumption is that healthy people build healthy programs. So the health of these people is a first priority. When I've watched programs suffer, a few strategic questions usually uncover the real issue...someone's life is falling apart.

"But am I my brother's keeper?" we quote Cain, who killed Abel in the early chapters of the Bible's Genesis story.

God's answer to that question, from Genesis to Revelation, is an emphatic: **"Yes, as a matter of fact, you are."**

How we define keeper, of course, is key. My belief is that we are all accountable to one another and keepers of each other's spiritual and emotional health. A *keeper*—as in the case of a zookeeper—feeds, nurtures and protects the animal *from others* and others *from that animal*. It is not rude or meddling to ask someone, "How are you?" and to build a relationship that solicits an honest, thorough answer.

A Lesser Kind of Intervention

But what if basically healthy people are simply performing poorly, or they've tried something that isn't working? What if Tom Sawyer looked up and saw that his whitewashers were using purple paint or creating a streaky finished product?

Sometimes, an intervention is merely programmatic and performance-based. "I've given you a long rope on this project and, sad to say, it isn't working. It's time to change direction." I consider this a **"small i" intervention**. It isn't really that serious—just a course correction. My position or perspective allows me to see the need for change clearly, while my associate is too close for perspective or stubbornly committed to something that isn't working.

The challenge in this kind of intervention is to sustain the associate's sense of freedom, creativity and trust. It seems important to say, "This idea or program isn't meeting up to my hopes, but I still have high hopes for you. Make the necessary adjustments and keep going." I can't guarantee that the associate won't walk with a limp for awhile, but if I encourage in believable ways, the limp shouldn't last.

The challenge in a volunteer organization is this: failing volunteers will hesitate to volunteer ever again. This is one excellent reason to **enlist volunteers for fixed blocks of time.** If things go south, their end-of-term will arrive in the nick of time, sparing them embarrassment and affording us the chance to bring in some new blood. Celebrate their efforts and then replace them.

The best intervention for volunteers, though, is to send reinforcements—to enlist more people to come alongside. Even broken strategies can have good outcomes if enough good-hearted people are working the program.

For example, the first youth retreat I ever organized was shoddy and ill-conceived. We had too many rambunctious urban junior-highers in a cabin in the mountains without space for them to romp. The experience was clunky at best and dangerous at worst. Policing the teens was exasperating. Teaching and campfire times were constantly interrupted. I felt like a failure—until their hearts opened up. Those urban teens had a life-changing experience. Our ill-conceived but good-hearted efforts made a real difference in those young lives.

Why? How?

Through it all, these adolescents were surrounded by several adults who cared for them, even when the teens assaulted us with bad behavior. What we lacked in strategy or expertise, we compensated for with hearty good intent and a hand-full of volunteer reinforcements.

A Breach in Core Values

The most frequent interventions tend to surround breaches of core values.

- If **integrity** is a core value, sometimes we have to intervene and steer an associate out of the gray.

- If **excellence** is a core value, sometimes we have to intervene when someone is getting sloppy.

- If **high-authorization** is a core value, sometimes we have to intervene when an associate is micromanaging—limiting the scope of impact by *juggling* balls instead of "getting the ball into the hands of people who can make plays."

Intervention is hard. It requires *playing the heavy.* The best self-initiating, competent associates won't like interventions. They'll be embarrassed and sometimes angry. Interventions always hurt and some of us tend to get angry when we're hurt or embarrassed. But most of the best will need an occasional intervention.

Learn from the Master

Since intervention can be delicate work, I try to learn from history's greatest leader. In sticky situations, Jesus asked questions. Better than offering definitive observations or directives, he made people think and own their own beliefs and actions.

In one case, Jesus is being upbraided by leaders for pronouncing forgiveness to a disabled man. "Who does this Jesus think he is? God?"

Jesus answers their outrage with a rhetorical question. "Which is easier? To forgive this man or to heal him?" The question draws the religious leaders into a more reflective mode—then Jesus heals the man. And forgives him!

With well-crafted questions, even an intervention can turn into a positive, reflective collaboration, rather than risking adversarial or defensive feelings.

"How do you perceive your situation?" I might ask. "Are you succeeding according to your hopes, or has this been a disappointing season?"

That's not to say that we should be evasive. **People need to know the truth and deal with it.**

Still, there are *ways* to tell the truth that make it palatable and even inspiring. If we love the power trip too much, we prefer to *just say it and let them deal with it.* That might work for some people, but not most. Injured people will even turn on us and begin galvanizing support from others, creating a mutiny.

When Necessary, Get Tough

Some associates might need us to be very firm and use a strong tone. In one tough scenario, I tried almost everything to intervene for one associate over a period of years. When we finally ended his employment, he indicated confusion. "I didn't know things were that serious."

Exasperated, I asked, "How can you say that? We've had dozens of talks. I've even used the word *probation* during two different seasons. I find myself doing constant interventions."

His answer? "But you never even raised your voice."

His leadership style was to *get mean* when he was truly serious. So he was waiting for me to get mean. Because I failed to rant and rave, he assumed I was only mildly concerned about his situation.

That's not to say that I'm going to start getting mean. At the very least, though, I could have looked him straight in the eye and said, "It's not my way to get nasty, but you need to know how deadly serious I am right now. Your employment hinges on your ability to hear me right now and to change."

Of course, that's almost exactly what I did on more than one occasion. He did not, from my view, understand that language. Perhaps he needed to work in a context that spoke *his language* better than I did. Or, as it turned out, he just needed a fresh context for success. He found it and flourished completely.

Relationship is the Key

The best platform for the best intervention is real relationship.

Some disagree with a relational approach to leadership and recommend a professional distance. No personal interest. No lunches together. Leave home and marriage and faith and hobbies out of the office. That distance, they say, creates respect and respect gives authority. That distance, they say, is necessary for objectivity and, when necessary, confrontation and even dismissal.

I hear that caution and see the benefits. If I'm only a boss or supervisor, and not a friend, I might feel less sheepish and feel more freedom to give correctives or ask for more effort or excellence. If this is purely and only an employee, his or her feelings are only important to the degree that they affect performance. **I'm not as likely to be hurt** or disappointed by an employee who falls short of hopes. And it might pain me less to remove a failing employee.

But I don't want employees. I want associates. I still prefer to risk those pains for the sake of seeing associates as real comrades, friends and fellows.

Yes, friendship can muck up the works in the hard times; but the benefits of camaraderie on the morale of the total enterprise are irrefutable. I want people to work *with* me, not *for* me.

"Are you saying that friendship is a ploy to lead people better for the sake of corporate success?"

No. It is important for people to care about people and help one another succeed for the best of reasons. Life is not so compartmentalized. Viewed as an integrative whole, it seems best to invest in the entire person. Call it idealistic, but I choose to care about the people I share life with.

And, yes, it's good business to care.

For the Chronic Challenge

Again, some people require constant intervention. What should we do? Sometimes, we might feel called to a long-suffering relationship that requires a huge investment in coaching and care.

- Perhaps this person has outstanding upsides
   and the overall contribution is worth the pain.

- Perhaps this person needs us during a season of personal loss or emotional struggle. We exercise patience and hope for better days.

- Or this is a trainee and we really believe that enough investment will bear fruit over the long haul.

Or we just have to pull the plug on this draining situation. It's likely that some other employment will make the person happier and be a better fit. Or the crisis of unemployment might be the last straw that forces someone to look in the mirror, get real help and get retooled for a more positive season elsewhere.

One piece of advice learned the hard way: it's best to **keep a paper trail of serious interventions**, even obtaining signatures from the associate indicating, "I have heard and read and understand the changes being asked of me and the serious consequences if changes are not successful."

Whether these interventions take place during a standard review cycle or between reviews, they serve as protection for everyone. When I've neglected to record interventions and demand a sign-on, I've had associates say, "You never told me that!" Or, "Everything has been fine, and *now* you're asking me to leave?" It has astonished me how forgetful some people can become about interactions that affect them so completely.

Remember the Broader Implications

Remember, interventions threaten to create splashes that turn into waves that gather momentum in ever-growing *tsunamis*.

One for-profit executive told me, "The tough thing for you non-profit leaders is that when you come down hard on one person, an entire group comes down hard on you. It can sour the whole organization. In business, it doesn't work that way. If I fire one person and the person in the next desk complains, I fire that person, too. You can't exactly do that, can you?"

No. So sometimes the best way to do an intervention is with an entire group. I use what I call "listening sessions" to create dialogue and open the door for hard truths to be exchanged. Then I try to model honesty and health in both the telling and the listening.

Ticklish Business

So intervention is the most ticklish part of the high-authorization model and the part we always hope to avoid. Sometimes we can avoid intervention for long periods by being attentive and proactive in our accountability. Still, the day for intervention will come. It will be hard. It won't be fun. Intervention is best done with much prayer.

Here are more helpful cues toward successful interventions:

1. ***Don't drop a bomb.*** *Give the associate an opportunity to prepare. "We have some hard things to discuss. Can you meet with me later today?" This allows time to eat, pray or otherwise brace up for the encounter. And don't leave this overnight; or if you must, no more than a night or two. Some people behave badly by rallying allies or raising a storm of self-protective counter maneuvers. This is how wars can start in companies and, yes, even in churches.*

2. **The setting matters.** *I usually choose to intervene in a setting that's more familiar to my associate. As hard as it is to be a bearer of bad tidings, it is much tougher on the receiving end. If an overly emotional reaction is likely, a public place affords a check on elevated emotions.*

3. **Include a third person.** *I place the third party beside the associate, facing me. This presents a posture of advocacy for my associate, instead of the perception of being ganged up on. If I'm intervening with a woman, the third party should be another woman. If I were a woman, I would ask a man to sit with us, whether my associate is a man or woman. Someone might find a way to make that sound gender-offensive; I'm simply trying to disarm potentials for misunderstanding and I don't want to be a bully with the authority that my position entails.*

4. *Be specific, clear and brief. Provide data, examples, honest observations and clear action steps.*

5. *Give the associate time to process this information and respond in a seasoned way. Allow for emotional reactions. Some people appear okay in the face-to-face setting and then go blow off steam. Others rant and rave or behave defensively; but with a little bit of time, they come around to a more productive response. None of us are machines. Hard news hurts.*

6. *Follow up. Make sure that mutual understanding has been reached and that real steps are in place for improvement. Give clear deadlines and metrics for measuring change. Make sure that the associate is still "in the game" emotionally.*

7. *Prayer really helps; anywhere, anytime.*

Which leads to the next piece of the model.

Chapter Thirteen

Prayer: I Want the Best for You

Prayer changes things. Prayer changes people. Prayer changes the person doing the praying. Prayers are answered. God hears. God cares. God intervenes. Not always in the way we hope. Not always in the timing we hope for. But God is real and prayer makes a difference.

You might not share those convictions. Still, in my leadership approach, prayer is critical. Telling an associate, "I'm committed to praying for you," communicates a number of things. "Your overall well-being is a priority. I care about the whole person, even your family. There are aspects to your success beyond my control (even your control) and I'll advocate for you before God."

Even for Those Who Don't Pray

Even for those who don't practice or believe in prayer, there's something powerful about saying (authentically), "I wish you well. And there's more to it than wishing you would be a highly productive contributor to the business." If that's all we really hope for—worker productivity—this entire model springs a leak. If people are no more than cogs and pawns, it's better to build a model of low-authorization and high-control, and then hire people who take orders, give orders and generally want to punch in, punch out and make a profit. Those aren't the kind of people I want with me and I'm probably not the best cash cow for them.

Caring Matters

This model is built on genuine care. It assumes that people matter. Mutual respect, as a common attitude and behavior, fuels every aspect of the model. Wanting *the best* for one another is a given. Competition is fine as a mutual stimulant, but not as a way of self-advancement at the expense of others. Conflict is an unavoidable part of sharing space and dividing resources, but even conflict needs resolution, forgiveness and, ultimately, the birth of deeper community.

This model is all about life together. And all of us, hopefully, want to *do life well*. Even Tom Sawyer, who seems too childishly narcissistic to actually care about others, proves to be generous and even heroic later in the story.

So I care for my associates. And in caring, I also pray. Not as often as I could or as fervently as I might intend. But I pray for them, for their spouses and emerging relationships, and for their children and grandchildren. I pray for their crises and for their vacations. I pray for their golf outings and for their internal peace. I'm not sure I can document improving golf scores, though friends have told me, "I've had my best rounds when I've played with you."

This I know: the people I work with have almost universally celebrated the pleasure and peace that pervade our work environment. I believe that prayer is central to creating that environment.

Sending and Receiving

Sometimes, people leave. More than once, I've been accused of being cavalier about the departure of co-workers. As they left our enterprise for different reasons, I was enthusiastic about their new adventures and optimistic about incoming replacements. Asked, "Why can you so easily dismiss them? Aren't you sorry or grieving at all about this change?"

My answer, spoken or unspoken, is this: "I've been praying for this departing person for a long time. I trust God's sovereignty and I trust this person's freedom and sense of God's leading. If it's good for Joe to leave, it's going to be good for *us* that Joe leaves. I'm eager to meet the next member of our team. I'm eager to enjoy the distinctive contributions that the new person will make. I'm even eager to enlarge my sense of family by one more person or one more family. I'm eager to make a new friend."

Some people might say, "A new friend? Yuck! How can you muddy business with pleasure? Why would you confuse working relationships with friendship?"

Oh, why not! We're here such a short time! My deathbed conversations with highly confessional people rarely sound like this: "I wish I'd made fewer friends and more money. I wish I'd been more objective and cut-throat about the business. I wish I'd made more investments in product and less in people."

On the contrary, those confessions go more like this: "I wish I'd been more attentive, more available, more relational and more prayerful."

The Truth About Leaders

As leaders, **we have *so much real power* to make the lives of other people better.** How we responsibly leverage that power is the real stuff of stewarding the gift of life; and our gifts of leadership and influence.

In Charles Dickens' *A Christmas Carol*, Ebenezer Scrooge makes life miserable for his associate, Bob Cratchit. Scrooge pays poor wages. The working conditions are bleak. The emotional environment is cold and demeaning. Cratchit stays in Scrooge's employ only out of desperate need. He has a large family and a sick child (Tiny Tim). Scrooge is unconscionably inconsiderate of Cratchit's well-being.

As part of Scrooge's program for redemption, the Ghost of Christmas Past takes Scrooge back to his own early employment with Mr. Fezziwig. Fezziwig brought a jolly goodwill to work. His Christmas parties were legendary. His interest in his employees was genuine. Fezziwig's contrast with Scrooge as an employer is stark. Fezziwig knew how to live!

And how to lead.

Scrooge learns his lessons well. The *new* Scrooge gives Cratchit a huge raise and sets out to find the doctors who can save Tiny Tim. He forgives debtors and begins investing in the help and hope of the community.

A Responsibility From God

This is my assumption: **anyone gifted by God with the ability to lead, build an enterprise, make money or otherwise affect the course of many lives *has also been given responsibility*.**

Again, I'm not responsible *for* everyone, but I am responsible *to* them—I'm responsible to use my God-given gifts for the common good. Whether I'm blessed with resources or intellect or creativity or motivation or energy or training or education or position, my assumption is this—I'm *blessed to be a blessing.*

This notion is at the core of the Judeo-Christian ethic. In *Genesis* 12:1-3, God tells Abraham (the "father" of those two great religions), "I'm going to bless you and your offspring to be a blessing to all the world." That **other-consciousness is a building block of any worthy life philosophy and leadership approach.**

The great malady of our culture of leaders is that **greater success often leads to greater insulation and isolation from the real needs of real people:**

- We leverage our power and status to separate ourselves and to create oases of comfort and privilege.

- We think we've earned the right to avoid the messiness of other lives.

- We think we've paid our dues on the way up and can leave the blights and plights of humanity for other schmucks.

We're wrong. Dead wrong. Whatever our view of God or humanity, that kind of thinking is just so sad, so antisocial and so narcissistic.

And it does absolutely nothing to grow us into the kind of leaders our associates can't wait to follow.

Whatever ghosts you need to send, Lord, to wake up our slumbering consciences, please send them soon. This world is a mean, s*orrowful place filled with so many beautiful people whose lives could be so much better.*

And they have so much to offer us in real friendship and meaningful partnership. *Lord, help us to make all of our lives richer.*

Whitewashing the Fence

Lord, teach us to pray.

Chapter Fourteen

Provision: I'll Get You What You Need

The best associates need the best kind of advocates; especially bosses who are *for* them. If we want them to succeed, they need resources, staff and incentive.

As for resources, the best people deserve the chance to prove their expertise and savvy. That means putting tools in their hands and money at their disposal to take risks and venture out.

Tom Sawyer didn't ask his friends to finger-paint the fence. He was resourceful and committed enough to make sure that they had the brushes and the paint and whatever else they needed for the job.

Of course, executives are always working with finite resources. As I write this version of the book, our economy is creeping slowly out of the worst crisis since The Great Depression. Almost everyone has had to downsize and pinch pennies. And I doubt that this is the last time.

Working with Limited Resources

In the non-profit world, this is tough. We're working with limited money that comes from the benevolence of generous people. Sometimes, contributors feel strong emotional ties to the organization and fear aggressive spending that might put the whole at risk. Most contributors, especially in churches, have a conservative view regarding how their money should be spent and have no idea how much it costs to produce a quality program or great materials. If programs skimp on spending, constituents bemoan the lack of quality. If programs spend on quality, others bemoan the lavish expenditures. Most of the time, people are simply ill-informed or out-of-date regarding real costs and current methodologies.

For example, my most recent organization had stark, utilitarian printed materials that smacked of archaic, institutional biases—an accurate impression in the early days of my tenure. When we gave our newly commissioned Communication Team the authorization and resources to improve logo, branding and the whole communication effort, the team answered the call. Most of our materials became more attractive, current, readable and engaging. Our processes were updated and streamlined. Almost everything improved.

But it took no time at all for the *other* voice to cry out, "How could you spend that kind of money?" And some even declared that they would withhold their giving "if you're just going to waste it."

That voice doesn't realize: If even one household is touched because of our attractive brochures and promotional pieces *and then joins*, the entire upgrade has been paid for. Even more, the materials themselves are more likely to attract and engage scads of people in a culture where quality matters.

Dynamic, on-the-move organizations know this. They understand the concept of seed money. Sometimes it takes money upfront to reach people, knowing that a byproduct of reaching more people will be more money; and more money allows us to reach still more people.

Even beyond money issues, the conservative voice doesn't realize that the best people will want to produce the best product or service. So they need **the best available resources for success**. For example, one of my employers hired a time-tested, energetic youth pastor. As he negotiated employment, he said, "In order to succeed, I need money and staff and allocated space so that I can build the program you're asking for." It was a hard swallow for business-as-usual types; but the benefits of this associate's efforts were obvious and numerous. Without the resources he asked for, he simply never would have come. We would have settled for someone with less experience and a smaller vision.

And by the way, institutional thinkers complained about his strategy during his entire tenure, even when the fruit popped out all over the place.

To use another example, Isaac Stern played a Stradivarius violin to produce the finest possible sound to complement his skills and training. He probably could have made a dime-store violin sing; but he wouldn't tolerate a cheap instrument for long.

Honoring and Sustaining Excellence

I'm interested in sustainability, convinced that keeping great people for sustained seasons safeguards success. My experience indicates that the best programs have been built by the best people over many years. I'm also interested in being the kind of person who recognizes character and talent, draws them out and honors them. It's not about me.

Occasionally during budget crunches **I've had to tell associates, "We have to produce a lot with a little."** For short bursts of time, this is possible, and even refreshing. Sometimes creativity is born out of Spartan resources and sometimes the importance of relationship surfaces during seasons that are less reliant on resources. But even during tight times, associates need the hope that one day they'll be operating with all the essential tools, instead of something less. Without that hope, they will likely move on to greener pastures.

The other side of provision is **remuneration.** Again, in the non-profit world, funds are limited and the donor mindset is generally conservative. Though the pay might be less compared to equal work and expertise in other fields, I need to be prepared to advocate upper-end salaries if I want top-level associates. In the non-profit world, no one jumps in to make big money. Few people are greedy. Nonetheless, the best associates need to feel that they and their families are cared for.

And that their contributions are appreciated. **Most of us attach symbolic value to our paychecks.** Money equals tangible appreciation. More money means even more appreciation. Less money equals less appreciation and might be interpreted as a subtle reproof.. Whether it *should* be that way or not, people *feel* this. **When income growth is static, people assume that their contributions to the organization are modest at best.** They will doubt themselves and their value in the organization.

Funds are also limited in the for-profit world. Paing top salaries isn't easy anytime or anywhere. In either realm, it's better to pay more money for the right people than for any other ingredient. Finding and appreciating the right people in actual, tangible ways is critical.

An Advocate and a Fellow

So associates need to feel my advocacy. And if there are seasons when they need to sacrifice (no raises, for example), they need to see that I'm not advancing without them. Pay affects morale. Inequities affect morale.

I know of one pastor's family that was told by church leaders, "We don't want you to get out ahead of the people financially." Then, at meeting after meeting, the pastor was hosted by church leaders in large, beautiful homes that the pastor's family would never be able to afford. The phrase "We don't want you to get out ahead of the people" became a private refrain in the pastor's family that basically meant, "You hypocrites!" Morale suffered until the incongruity was resolved. Money matters. It's practically helpful and symbolically loaded.

Other things affect morale:

- **Opportunity** affects morale.

- **A positive, familial work environment** will *keep* people here who've been offered more money elsewhere.

- The **competence of "management"** affects morale.

- The **humanity of "management"** affects morale.

- **The promise of doing something worth doing** is the best attraction of all for the best people.

All of those benefits flow freely in this high-authorization model. Under these working conditions, people tend to feel rich and free.

Real Help and a Clear Runway

Another critical provision is support staff. Most of the best leaders are mobilizers—they conjure dreams and visions for programs that require many hands and heads to operate. They need freedom to bring in some of their own people.

This might involve **"cleaning house" before the arrival of the new associate,** so that he/she will have freedom to build a staff that fits his/her vision. While the new associate must embrace a host of pre-existing values and visions in the resident environment, everyone must allow some space for a new person to bring a personal signature. That often means replacing a few people.

In the world of sports, this is commonplace. When a head coach is replaced, the assistant coaches keep their bags packed. It's possible the new coach will keep them for reasons of compatibility or consistency. It's far more likely that **the new coach will want a fresh beginning with new assistants who have no ties to the old ways of doing things.**

The new person should not have to face the ominous emotional task of firing people (paid or volunteer) during the honeymoon. And if future staff needs are uncertain, people need to be coached to let go of expectations and stand by, ready for a new way of doing things. Employment might be tenuous until future needs are established. **If feelings are hurt by displacement, better that I should be saddled with blame than the new associate.**

Once, while clearing the runway for a new full-time associate, I had to remove part-time and volunteer workers who had relentless ties to old ways of doing things. While I suffered their reactions and those of their sympathizers, I had the organizational position and emotional wherewithal to withstand the backlash. I didn't wish that backlash to land on the newcomer, who arrived with the freedom to build his own team. **One great provision for a new associate is a clear runway** to land on, along with enough space to launch new things in new ways.

Provide Administrative Help

Many of the best leaders have blind spots in the realm of administrative detail. We can either bemoan their shortfalls or staff for their shortfalls. Remember:

- Bemoaning gets us nowhere.

- Staffing to fill deficits can free up a talented associate to make huge gains.

- Increasing the amount of his/her time and energy devoted to primary gifts and passions helps everyone.

- Minimizing the amount invested in secondary talents or deficits boosts enjoyment, and enjoyment is so often the key to exceptional gains.

This process of maximizing strengths and minimizing the negative impact of weaknesses requires the best use of every good resource. I've used *Please Understand Me,* by David Keirsey and Marilyn Bates[56], in

---

[56] Keirsey, David and Marilyn Bates. *Please Understand Me:*

all of my staff cultures. This excellent book utilizes the Myers-Briggs personality test to identify types and tendencies so that people understand well where their greatest strengths and vulnerabilities lie; and also those of their co-workers. Mutual understanding so often lessens the potential for disappointment and tension.

As for my own deficits, **I try to remind those who bemoan them, "My deficit is your calling. This thing about me that frustrates you is the on-ramp to your success.** Be completely who you are, and try not to waste energy wishing my weaknesses away." In the hardest moment, I might even say, "If I didn't have this deficit, I wouldn't need you. But I DO need you. Please, don't try to change me. Compliment me!"

To some leaders, this chapter is upside down. "The employee's job is to provide exactly what I ask!"

I simply believe in **reciprocity and servant-leadership.** If I provide the pieces necessary for my associates' success, they're more likely to provide quality work and an excellent product. Together, we raise the tide.

Character & Temperament Types. Del Mar:
    Prometheus Nemesis Book Company, 1984.

Chapter Fifteen

Protection: *I've Got Your Back*

With authorization comes protection—especially if I want bold leaders and risk-takers to catalyze real movement. And I want aggressive vision-casters. I want them to feel honored and safe enough to *dare*. I try to foster the spirit of adventure that portends invention and innovation. "You go for it. I've got your backside."

Then, beyond verbal assurances, risk-takers need proven protection. They need to actually see me protecting them while they stick their necks out.

Spread the Credit, Own the Blame

This is not intended to sound heroic—just smart. When a bold associate succeeds with innovative programs, that associate should get the credit. Many times,

I've heard people lament about their bosses, "I did this thing, but he took all the credit. He's acting like he did it himself."

Of course, a CEO or primary leader will ultimately carry the load of both blame and acclaim.

But I want my associates to enjoy sharing the acclaim with little concern for blame. Carrying downside potential is part of the mantle of my leadership position.

So if the program fails, I take the blame. After all, I authorized this person and urged aggressive behavior. If things go south, it happened on *my* watch, under *my* direction. It's part of my role to assume that risk. Honestly, **assuming that I can find and hire outstanding people, the only thing that separates us enough to justify my higher salary is my willingness to bear a larger burden.** The difference certainly isn't skill or intellect.

Providing an Umbrella

In his book, *Who's Holding the Umbrella*,[57] Bill Yaeger describes life *under the umbrella* as a safe place to take chances and establish a personal style.

Some leaders require associates to adopt a regimented style and approach that bears all the marks of the company culture. I prefer wide, high, clearly marked guardrails that offer both freedom and confidence. **People take more and better risks when they feel both safe and free.** My goal is to maintain widely held core values and overarching goals, but give emerging leaders the freedom and security to add their own signatures to their work—*to our work*. This fosters more creativity and longer tenures among happier associates.

There are ways to *opt out* from the protective

---

[57] Yaeger, William E. *Who's Holding the Umbrella*. Nashville: T. Nelson Publishers, 1984.

shelter of the umbrella:

- **Ethical/moral failure**. The degree and type of moral or ethical failure might have more or less serious consequences in different organizations or roles, but it's always catastrophic.

- **Insubordination**. I love mavericks and people with some swagger, but a high-authorization culture requires respect. It has to travel both ways.

- **Disrespect for others**. We're building a team. People who are dismissive or destructive toward others are misfits.

- **Incompetence**. Again, if I hire an incompetent person, it's my fault. But it still means that changes are coming. I'll try to be fair and even make a space somewhere else in the organization where flaws are not exposed. But sometimes people overreach and overpromise and they interview much better than they perform.

- **Laziness**. We simply need hard working, focused people who enjoy showing up and diving in.

Realize, there are gradations of all the above. Everyone has bad days and tough times, and all of us have great strengths and serious weaknesses. Still, those unsafe behaviors put all protection—the whole organization—at risk.

Protection From Hasty Dismissal

Numerous or egregious failings will certainly put employment at risk in any organization. But in a high-authorization culture that honors protection, there shouldn't be any surprises. Accountability with a commitment to relationship opens many opportunities for honest interaction about "how things are going." Before someone loses employment—hopefully long before—there would be enough conversations and interventions to pave the way out the door for reasons that have become obvious; or to pave a path toward reassignment to an area where success is more likely.

Protecting Reputations and Hire-ability

Even in painful dismissals mentioned earlier in the book, I protected associates more than they ever knew. I protected reputations and hire-ability. I helped them find excellent new positions. I didn't have to lie or even stretch the truth. Their new employers were undeterred by their frailties (we all have them) and I was free to highlight their many talents. I truly believed they would flourish in new environments.

All the while, I absorbed the criticism from those in our organization who rose up to advocate for the departed, believing that my own position and reputation could survive the onslaught. For the most part, they did. As one close advisor told me in the midst of *dismissal backlash*, "Just float. You'll be fine. Don't defend yourself or smear the departed. Just float."

Share Holders are Opinion Holders

That, by the way, is a unique challenge in leading volunteer organizations. Unpaid "employees" and "shareholders" are opinion-holders. Usually, people are quite free with those opinions, even when they are uninformed and harm the organization.

And in any organization, if we've hired strong people we've hired people with strong views. There has to be a sense that people can speak into the decisions that affect them, their peers and their programs.

But there are limits to how far we let that go. Too many opinions from too many directions can have a poisonous effect. **Protect your associates even from the burden of making judgments and decisions in arenas that aren't their direct responsibility.**

Not that bosses don't make mistakes. So if we really want our associates to enjoy confidence and freedom, we want them to assume that any radical actions (demotions, dismissals) are the product of long deliberation and frequent conversation. I don't want to treat their trust carelessly or betray it by being rash. I want to protect staff from the fear of impulsive, harmful executive behavior and secure for them the greatest possible
chance for success.

In one case, I inherited several associates when I answered a call to lead a large organization. The entire staff handed me their virtual resignations, communicating their willingness to create a clean runway for me.

I received their open spirit with gratitude and took time to observe the staff. A season of observation showed me that one associate was losing energy for his role. He'd served beautifully in the interim, but my hopes for that role were different than his capacity in that role. He knew. I knew. So we created a new position where he served much more effectively. He flourished, outgrew that role and moved on to become a hugely successful lead executive in another organization.

Protection From Themselves

Even then, his departure was painful. The more competent he became, the more he questioned my decisions—sometimes for good reason! Almost like an individuating teenager, he bucked against me. While this created its own set of issues and hurts, we worked hard to protect each other. He tried to process his disappointments with safe people outside the immediate organization. And I protected him through his growing agitation by helping to secure an excellent position where he could keep growing—and do it *his way*.

To great effect, I should add. In a new setting, he was able to create a leadership culture with his own signature and style. In a new place and role, he had even more freedom to be completely himself—a tremendous leader.

All in all, **the greatest benefit of high-level protection in a high-authorization culture is freedom**. Associates are free to innovate, experiment and expand into hugely successful contributors. They're even free to leave with a blessing. If their departure comes during obvious successes, they leave our organization with morale high and the machinery in place to sustain good things. If they leave during down times, the door flies open for new people and potential renewal in the organization.

Protection From Criticism

Sometimes, protection means guarding associates from the criticism of others. Excellent people suffer deflating blows to morale when they feel disrespected or misunderstood by people they are trying to serve. They also suffer confusion when they don't know how much credence to give to the criticisms or suggestions of others in the organization.

Toward that end, I tell associates, "Primarily, you work *with* me. But when you need to understand or benefit from clear lines of authority, you work *for* me. In *principle*, you serve God. In *spirit*, you serve everyone. But in *practice*, **you work for me**. Not the Board. Not the whims and hues and cries of the mob. You work for me."

Most people are hungry for that kind of clarity. Role confusion and hazy lines of authority steal energy. If that clarity creates conflict ("But these people I work with every day see things a different way! It's exhausting to manage their change resistance!"), then we problem-solve together. "How do we bring people along? Would it be helpful for me to talk personally with that constituency? Do we need sweeping changes in personnel in that area?"

No matter what, I don't want my associate too troubled by conflicting loyalties. "You work for me."

Protection From Ambiguity

If that "you work for me" talk sounds like a power trip, it isn't. In the right moment, it brings clarity and freedom. Among a host of morale drains (gossip, loss of a beloved leader or associate, financial woes, insufficient administrative or financial support...), the greatest drain on morale comes from ambiguity. *Who do I answer to? Who should I try to please? Who should I not be trying to please?*

If I want my associates to be innovators, that means protecting them from the not-so-helpful input of nice people who are prone to resist change and guard mediocre familiarity.

To borrow a football image, the best associates need a leader willing to be a *pulling guard*, clearing away defenders and mowing down opposition.

In one of my current roles, I'm an associate. Every day, I draft on the leadership of our CEO. Every day, I enjoy the confidence of knowing that as long as I'm serving his purposes effectively, my employment is secure and my work has value. In fact, his **steady advocacy gives me courage and enthusiasm to make necessary changes**, even with the knowledge that some changes won't be popular.

As a rule, I don't want associates to even know or feel the opposition. I'd rather have them **operating in a naïve bubble of freedom,** living under the assumption that other people love what they're doing. I try to carefully screen and filter the comments that others make about them. If the criticism is accurate, then I create a teaching moment and **the criticism comes from me.** But I don't want them defending themselves against numerous faceless objectors and antagonists. That's exhausting and demoralizing.

One Exception

There are exceptions learned the hard way. For example, I realized that at times **I've protected my associates too much from each other**. This well-intended vigilance on my part contributed to what some would call "the silo effect." After being exposed to the writings of Patrick Lencioni,[58] I know that I contributed to independent domains of influence with little cross-pollination or mutual accountability.

---

[58] Lencioni, Patrick. *Silos, Politics and Turf Wars: A Leadership Fable About Destroying the Barriers That Turn Colleagues Into Competitors.* San Francisco: Jossey-Bass. 2006

This led to frustration. Some associates harbored feelings of every kind—resentment, jealousy, disrespect—toward other associates without the freedom to voice their concerns or test their observations. "Can't one department question the viability of another? "

I've learned to lower my guard and actually **encourage free and feisty conversations between associates**. And even allow them to challenge me!

In the immediate, this feels risky. In the long run, this honesty creates a safer, more open community. That community lends toward emotional freedom to innovate, build and grow. As a result, they'll build something that fewer people can ultimately criticize.

And if they can't build such a thing?

Then I hired and authorized the wrong people—and that's *on me*. It's my responsibility. I'll intervene, intervene, intervene. Over time, things will get better or changes will be made.

Protection During Hard Seasons

Sometimes, protection means guarding associates during seasons of fatigue, depression or personal loss. When I've **stayed with associates and *stood up for them* during hard times, the result has almost always been gratitude, loyalty and long-term gain.**

Those seasons have been caused by events like the loss of loved ones, unexpected depression or illness, marital difficulty or midlife crisis.

Sometimes, **I've protected older, good-hearted, legacy staff,** simply because they deserved the opportunity to finish noble careers while enjoying the respect of others. I might trim down their responsibilities and hand over matters that need more energy and innovation. But I won't treat the "Tom Landry" types as shamefully as the Dallas Cowboys treated their legacy guy. Sure, they won Super

Bowls after discarding Landry. But they lost their status as "America's Team." Under Landry, people all over the country wore silver and blue Cowboy colors. After Landry's treatment, the team lost esteem in the eyes of the country, even while they claimed more Super Bowls. Whatever they won in rings, they lost in nationwide regard and esteem.

My own father was discarded by a company that he'd served for decades. During a sharp downturn in his industry, he was forced into "early retirement." He was told that his position was being discontinued. In truth, a young gun was hired to do much the same job under a new title for less money. Like so many other fifty-somethings, my dad had a hard time finding a similar position. Within two years, his heart stopped beating. I'm not the only one who feels that he died of a broken heart. I'm not suggesting that anyone should feel blame. But there are ways to handle legacy people with heart.

Our culture is mean to older people and discourteous about the honor that's due them. That's just one reason I'll carry a legacy person or two, and **enjoy the credibility capital** (before God and others) before I'll cast them out of the community. Better to remake their roles and let them mentor and sustain key relationships than lose their unique standing. Even more, **if legacy people are well honored, they end up running interference for me**. I *love* running behind bigger-than-life blockers.

One day, I'll be the legacy guy. **I'd rather set up a climate of grace, and then live in it, than establish a castoff culture and suffer for it.** I like to hope that someday others will protect me, since I've worked so hard to create a safe culture in which they can work and excel.

Section Three

Some Specific Applications

Whitewashing the Fence

Chapter Sixteen

Can a Leopard Change Its Spots?

Can a **micromanager** **become** a high-authorization leader?

My experience could make me a tad cynical. But **if change were impossible, I never would have written this book.** My concern is that most micromanagers are, by nature, not able to "let go and let God" or "let go and let others" or let go of anything.

That is not a put down. I am equally incapable of adopting micromanaging behavior. My assumption is that we need all types, and we need them well placed to be completely who and what they are. Some people should never change.

But the higher they go in an organization, the more micromanaging behavior will harm their chances at sustained success.

Most of us can't be categorized. We're still growing our leadership behaviors and we exhibit parts, pieces and gradations of types and tendencies.

That's all the more reason to flood the culture of the organization with reminders that this is our model. It seems best to create attractive (even funny) visual reminders, dramatic role-plays and good illustrations that teach and ingrain high-authorization behaviors.

How Do I Do This?

1. *Write all nine words of the high-authorization model on a whiteboard, blackboard, paper or overhead.*

2. *With one or all associates present, simply ask, "Which one of the AIPs do you need more of? Do you need more authorization, affirmation, accountability, information, ideas, intervention, prayer, provision or protection?"*

3. *Listen and let the associates dictate what, or how much, help is needed.*

4. *In some cases, at a staff meeting or in a personal interaction, an associate might say, "What I need isn't on the list. I need time." Or" I need rest." Or some other thing. Fine! The model isn't intended to be all-inclusive. It is, however, remarkably useful.*

5. *Encourage staff to provide the same model for their own associates. Some will turn around and offer the very same model.*

> *Others will adapt the model to something that better suits their personality, communication style or task at hand. Still, I want the same principles and practices to inculcate the organization.*

Time for Exceptions

There are exceptions. Some management-level associates are relentless micromanagers. I don't mean to use that word as a cuss word. I simply mean that some people are detail-oriented and have a highly directive leadership style. They also tend to hire people who love to take orders and fill orders. This is absolutely workable, especially at the production level, where innovation and self-initiation aren't necessarily called for. In that realm, micro-oriented leaders often produce the finest, quickest delivery of products by employing and managing diligent workers. We need people who are tenacious about details in order to provide the best possible goods and services.

There are also **highly creative, micromanaging leaders who are capable of rallying innovative efforts in short-term bursts of forceful energy.** These people are so often the best at leading task forces and pulling off big events—efforts with finite timelines.

But if the task or event drags on, micromanaging leaders often create friction and organizational wear-and-tear. Because of the tendency toward control, these leaders can often cross lines of authority, create a culture of negativity and impose their problem-solving, high dominance persuasions on a creeping scope of organizational terrain.

So, these valuable people need to be handled well—protected, really—from the downsides of their hard-driving tendencies. In the right contexts (projects of great importance over short duration) these prickly people can actually be superstars.

For example, I like to host meetings or conferences. Over the years, I've employed highly driven, detail-oriented people to gather and organize teams to pull off these significant events. When the event is over, the team is disbanded and the leader has succeeded. The goal is accomplished with great care before the opportunity arises for workers to be bruised or burned out.

Don't You Dare Devalue

For big-picture leaders who have a natural allergy against micromanagement, the tendency is to devalue detail-oriented people. It's far better to honor them and build them into the organization in ways that capitalize on their orientation. We really do need them. We just don't need them driving us or driving others crazy.

The sad reality is that big-picture people tend to devalue small-picture people, and vice versa. Relational people tend to devalue process-driven people, and vice versa. We simply must remember that all organizations need all types—at least, all constructive types. No one needs toxic or incompetent people.

Still, In Principle

For the most part, I want to hire leaders who are capable of giving their charges the same freedoms and protections I give them. If we want a high-authorization culture, then **key leaders need to own a high-authorization model**. I need associates who aren't going to give this model lip-service, or placate me by pretending to apply it to their areas of influence. I need them to own it and practice it, or else the culture of the organization will never benefit from the model. A few holdouts will forever create dangerous undertow by dragging people haplessly backward into tiring, dangerous surf.

When I arrived at one of my jobs, I was startled by the level of commitment to detail at high levels of leadership. People of good intent created notebooks on top of manuals on top of policies on top of spreadsheets on top of data, levers, bells and whistles of every kind. The smallest leadership initiatives required attention to a host of navigational tools and a steep path of exhausting orientation. Jumping through hoops and touching all the bases left me gasping for air long before reaching any real destination. The internal combustion created by all those starts, stops and steps of analysis and hyper-analysis left me desperate for relief. I'd come from a much more sophisticated, streamlined and accomplished environment, and all with much, much less effort. Something had to change in my new environment.

Day by day, year by year, these principles of high-authorization leadership began to take hold and bear fruit. Decisions were made more quickly. People learned to trust each other. Quality increased, as well as morale. Ideas morphed into products or services with very little resistance or friction. The sharp edge of politics fell away.

Yes, micro approaches to macro leadership were forever a fallback behavior that would periodically freeze the whole organization like a malevolent wrench in the cogs of progress. But the right voices would offer a history lesson and energies would be redirected again.

Again, About Non-Profits

The high-authorization model really works in volunteer organizations. Because the biggest turnoff to volunteers is wasted energy and effort, leaders must find ways to help volunteers feel useful and engaged. While some love to be given specific tasks, the real gains happen when volunteers feel called by God to steward their own aspirations. Those aspirations lead them into roles that have real scope and require skill and creativity.

Most volunteer organizations woefully under-employ great people, who end up fading to the periphery if their considerable gifts and experiences aren't well employed. Or they get recruited to serve on cautious boards where their innovative skills and decisive tendencies are thwarted by fearful, protective thinkers. And if they *are* invited to be self-initiating and innovative, nothing kills volunteer morale like others who can't resist impulsive meddling. Authorization and affirmation (the only paychecks a volunteer ever gets) work far better than micromanagement.

One man in one of my churches was a nationally known consultant who counsels huge non-profit groups through every kind of trial and opportunity. In our church, he was relatively unemployed until he felt called to invigorate our ministry of hospitality. I gave him a quick course in my values and visions, but he completely built a new ministry with his own signature and dozens of people alongside. He didn't need—and only occasionally wanted—my input. This was *his baby*. Micromanagement would have chased him away.

Still and Again, This Doesn't Mean Abdication

The other leadership risk with volunteers is abdication. While we want to authorize and give plenty of freedom, we still need to keep communication lines open and flowing. People need to know of our ongoing interest and accessibility. And, we need to be able to observe, ask questions and take a pulse.

More than once, I've honored the independence of volunteer leaders too much. Two bad outcomes have reared their ugly heads:

1. When the day came for the program or product to appear, the results were awful. In picking through the remains, I realized that I'd assumed too much and abdicated a partnership that could have been very useful. In short, the volunteers felt abandoned by me and the results were embarrassing for all of us.

2. Even the highly initiating leaders felt like I had dumped the whole thing into their laps. "Where did you go? One reason I agreed to do this was partnership. I wanted to do this with you, not without you."

I've tried to learn from both outcomes.

Relationship and Communication

How do we keep communication alive without meddling?

- *By being relational.*

- *By caring about the person.*

- *By walking around the whole operation so that people feel connected to us and, through us, to others.*

- *By creating group contexts where visions and values are reasserted over and over among each leadership level.*

If people aren't complaining about the tedium of hearing visions and values again and again, then we aren't recapitulating often enough. As much as people complain, they're more likely to forget if the driving visions and core values aren't constantly reintroduced.

To offset their complaints, **ask them to be the vehicles of delivering the visions and values in meetings.** That will cut the tedium and grow ownership in healthy ways.

And we don't just talk vision and values—we also need **to tell stories, care for each others' pains, celebrate successes and be community.**

The recapitulation makes leaders subject to some lampooning. All the better. The teasing and heckling—life together—will break down barriers of rank and hierarchy. Good structure and even lines of authority are necessary, but relationship creates blood flow in the organism that makes the whole body less brittle. We want real connections between people so that better communication and real accountability can sustain excellence in a high-authorization culture.

But What About My Authority?

What about respect? Note these definitions:

Leader: Someone people **choose** *to follow.*

Non-leader: Someone people are **forced,** *pressured or manipulated into following.*

If I need to wear my "Respect Me" badge to stroke my ego or to maintain order in the ranks, then I'm a propped-up figurehead, not a real leader. Furthermore, I'm likely over-employed and insecure. I probably need to make a career change to a role where I don't feel the pressure of forcing other people to respect and follow me.

There are exceptions. Sometimes, real leaders are called in to change a culture and accomplish the hard work of turning an organization around. It would be shocking to find a resistance-free zone. In fact, it would be normal to find sub-pockets of disrespect from "old guard" stalwarts who are waiting to be knighted by the new leader. Those people simply need to be moved out as swiftly as the culture can allow, or else they will infect the whole organization with negative energy and make your job pure hell as a leader.

All to say, don't bemoan the lack of respect or force respect. Remove disrespect using every available asset and all of the chips, trump cards and honeymoon grace you've been given in the early days.

But frankly, **if Tom Sawyer weren't already an established leader among peers, no one would have picked up a brush.**

Of course, even a leader people love to follow has to supervise and hold people accountable, often making hard decisions about programs and personnel. Relationships with associates can sometimes get sideways, requiring a reiteration of the lines of authority.

But if this is perpetual, the problem might be looking at us in the mirror. Not everyone is a leader. If you're not, don't force it. Find your place, enjoy your role, work hard and you'll end up being a leader by example. That wins honest respect anywhere in the world more than any title or position.

Whitewashing the Fence

Chapter Seventeen

High-Authorization Boards

One more critical application of this model: the relationship between boards and CEOs, and between boards and the staff culture.

The board-staff relationship is a tricky one to navigate. In truth, board work is not easy. How involved should board members be? What does real accountability look like in a day when corporations in America have suffered the worst kinds of ethical breakdowns—often because maverick CEOs have enjoyed too much autonomy?

While the pendulum is swinging back toward tighter board oversight, how much is too much before the CEO starts to squawk about meddlers and micromanagers?

Is our high-authorization model functional for this crucial role and relationship?

Yes. In fact, this model was created and refined by my own need to navigate a relationship as a CEO reporting to a Board of Directors.

- Because **the CEO's "boss" is a** *collective*, it's critical to define and refine the policies and behaviors that facilitate that relationship.

- Because I can't possibly work for numerous separate bosses, we've worked for years to clarify the ways in which their **collective discernment** finds form.

- Because I'm full-time, on-site, educated and highly experienced in leadership, **I share the responsibility of helping them lead me in a way that's authentic and useful.**

If I can't help them lead me in authentic ways, then they'll:

1. **Abdicate** and become passive figureheads, or

2. **Bottleneck**, micromanage and generally huff and puff to justify their position and authority. And I'll ignore or patronize them.

While patronizing or ignoring the board is standard operating procedure for many CEOs, it's not the best way to **enlist and sustain the finest board members, who really can be great contributors**. And it's not a smart way to utilize their individual and collective potentials. Boards really can help!

What I Need From the Board

So I go to the board and say, "This is what I need from you."

Authorization: I need freedom to do it my way. Many executives feel all of the responsibility, but also a lack of institutional authority. Please, authorize me to do what you hired me to do.

Affirmation: Your verbal encouragement means more than you can imagine. Because I respect you and your role, I care how you feel about my performance, and even about me. Cards, emails, phone calls and letters work well— and a generous paycheck speaks volumes.

Accountability: Keep me honest and keep me healthy. Healthy leaders lead healthy organizations. Ask the hard questions. Build a relationship that invites transparency. I'll do you the same favor, if you'll let me. Please, let's nurture a healthy organization together.

Information: Tell me the core values and visions that should drive and frame my work. Be visionaries with me and I'll find ways to make your dreams come true. Some of you predate me. What are the longstanding values and sacred behaviors that I must respect in order to flourish? Many things about this culture will be obvious to me, but I'll have my blind spots. Help keep me well-informed about your hopes so I can fulfill most of them.

Ideas: Feed me ideas, but please offer them in a free-handed way. You can imagine how many ideas I already have and how intuitive my leadership is. Still, go ahead. I'm listening. By the way, please send me, with your full blessing, to the places and people where the best ideas abound so I can be fully equipped.

Intervention: If I'm failing, in all or part of my role, please tell me quickly. Don't let me flounder alone. Don't wait until it's too late. Sometimes, I need a brave intervention. I have blind spots and I can swim in denial at times. Please, help.

Prayer: Please pray for me. Care for my health. Pray for my family. Care for my family. Their well-being can be as pivotal to my success as my own health.

Provision: Please figure out how to get me what I need to do what you've brought me here to do. I need a strong, healthy staff. I need streamlined decision-making structures. I need to know that my family's needs will be met. I need a vision-achieving and people-empowering budget. I need good administrative help. Please, don't send me out on an adventure without the proper equipment and team.

Protection: You've brought me here as an innovator

and instigator of change. Change will cause disruption and strong reactions. I need your protection . I am your visible arm, so I'm the one stuck out there in the range of fire. If I get pounded, we all suffer. I'm out on a limb. If you cut me off, we all suffer. Stand up for me. Guard my role. Defend my heart. Let's keep disagreements behind closed doors. Our unity will be a microcosm for the entire organization. You've got my back, right?

It's Tough to Teach UP

The challenge is in teaching this model *up*. It seems reasonable, sensible and practical. But some board members come onto the scene with egos, biases and behaviors that clog healthy attempts at collective discernment. Some bring expertise and longstanding experience. Many board members are retirement age, with fixed viewpoints and some cynicism about what they perceive to be new-fangled ways.

While experience lends obvious benefits, reticence about learning and practicing this high-authorization model will guarantee friction and dysfunction. At the very least, board members must be open to this approach, or else the holdouts will make the board/CEO relationship — and even the fellowship of board members—a painful misadventure.

I'm learning to do a much better job of **orienting new people and teaching the benefits** of this model with the help and leadership of existing board members.

I'm also more proactive in the selection process. Not that I want "yes people." I don't. I want strong, healthy people to supervise and oversee me; people strong enough to hold me accountable. But neither do I want micromanagers who try to insert their personal agendas and subvert the group process of collective discernment. I trust a collective of thoughtful people to arrive at a shared sense for what is wise and useful. I gladly submit to that collective, if I trust them.

If one board member hyper-extends himself and tries to act like my boss, I'm less likely to give as much weight to that one. **I'm not eager to fall in line with an uppity board member who disrespects group process and subverts the notion of collective discernment.** In other words, bullies don't make good board members no matter how smart they are. They chase fellow board members who are thoughtful introverts up against the wall and make honest, inclusive dialogue almost impossible. And bullies tend to micromanage.

In my decades of non-profit work, the most unsuccessful board members have often been "champions of industry" who were completely unaccomplished at group-think. Those hearty souls often earned their reputations by being assertive, decisive and bullish about their own style and philosophy of leadership. But in a group situation with co-equal standing, they've been frustrated and frustrating. They've come across as power-mongers—even when their motives were as pure as anyone else's.

One extraordinary exception was a man named Mel Bolin. Mel owned a large construction company and was the most influential person in our community. A strong, thoughtful leader, Mel established a culture of humility in the organization and among other leaders. On numerous occasions, he said to me, "You'll tell me, won't you, if I'm too big for the room? Don't let me have too much influence." He respected others and the necessity for a healthy group process. And though I was a young, upstart leader, he made me feel like an honored professional in my field. He was one of my own "personal Fezziwigs."

My most exhausting seasons in a quarter century of leadership came when I was challenged and thwarted by individual board members who acted on their own without the discernment and initiation of the entire council of voices. In the worst cases, the board would make decisions and set direction, and then one or two members would break rank and criticize and undercut the whole thing. **Boards must be united, cooperative and galvanized as they go public with their decisions.**

And as for *teaching up,* some board members will scorn this as impetuousness. In one situation, I arrived at a board meeting with ten copies of a book that I knew would enlarge and refine the vision of each and all members—and me! It was a proven book, with numerous and obvious helps, written by a prominent author.

Within days, one bullish board member informed me that I was out of line to present the books and impertinent to suggest that I had much of anything to teach him or others. In a few more days, I was able to gather the whole truth—two or three out of twelve agreed with him.

The great majority of board members were ready to learn and stretch together. But the first year with that organization was the most painful in all my years—until the day that small contingent quit rallying resistance.

So Can a Board Member Correct Me?

I *do* trust any one board member to speak into my life in corrective ways, *if we have a relationship.* If there's no relationship, I have no guarantee or confidence that the correction is valid or well-conceived. If we do have a relationship, then I can have confidence in a board member's particular areas of wisdom, experience and powers of observation.

However, **I will not receive that input as authoritative unless it comes from the collective board.**

From one member, I receive ideas or information as advice or perspective, and I measure its relative worth based on my assessment of that one person. When it comes from the whole group, I know that I should respond, either by accepting the counsel outright or else negotiating a common view.

I welcome input from people I know, trust and respect. And I trust and respect them more if they understand the limits of their own authority, experience and insight. Board members who huff and puff and overstep can create a sham that I can't play along with—a blustering board and a patronizing CEO. **Board members who love their power create low-authorization cultures that chase away the best leaders and stifle organizational growth and health.**

There might be CEOs who are willing to hop-to for overbearing boards, but they are more likely to perform as mere managers. Then the board will find themselves doing the work of a CEO. That requires a huge expenditure of time and effort and the likelihood of dysfunction everywhere.

One executive in a huge industry, who has also sat on numerous boards, told me, "Boards that try to manage things are inefficient. At best, they produce a minimum return on investment." **Boards that manage are fine for small and simple organizations, or for seasons of leadership transition.** But as things grow and become sophisticated, more leadership must be relegated to a CEO who actually likes to think and lead, and who has the time, staff, proximity and expertise to turn goals into reality.

John Carver's model provides useful distinctions between the extremes of working boards—that tend to be too hands-on—and deteriorating boards that have fully abdicated to the CEO. The healthy middle ground (what Carver calls *governance*) honors and respects the authorization and space that allows high-octane CEOs to excel. My high-authorization model is really one way to define and actualize Carver's healthy middle ground.[59]

The Critical Relationship of Board and CEO

Maintaining a healthy relationship between the board and CEO is *the one critical guarantor of success*.

Yes, some organizations flourish when the board is a figurehead function serving a patronizing CEO by staying out of the way. But abdication is as dangerous for boards as it is for CEOs. Huge public failures in the realm of corporate ethics should have taught us: boards need to be actual leaders, not figureheads. Worst-case scenarios abound, from Enron in the corporate sector to Jim Bakker in the religious. With no real accountability, strong CEOs can run amok.

And even healthy CEOs can be called away by illness, injury, death or a better offer, leaving an organization paralyzed—unless there is real leadership coming from the board.

So the board must be a genuine and practicing presence.

But **too much can be way too much**. I suppose that somewhere a micromanaging board is serving a growing organization; but that would, according to Carver, only be likely in the small, early, simple stages of organizational growth. Eventually, the organization is stifled by the board, or just ignores and outgrows an irrelevant board of frustrated, placated micromanagers. Either sounds sad to me. I'd rather have a board that adapts and serves well in every stage of growth.

So, this is what I suggest:

---

[59] Carver, John. *Boards that Make a Difference: A New Design for Leadership in Non-profit and Public Organizations.* San Francisco: Jossey-Bass, 2006.

1. *Make sure every board member **adopts this high-authorization philosophy**, or at least is willing to try it and test it.*

2. ***Create orientation experiences** so the CEO and board can dialogue freely about the principles and behaviors necessary to make this model effective.*

3. ***Add whatever language** or legal dimensions are necessary or specific for your setting.*

For example, when I walked into one leadership culture, staff associates didn't know who they worked for. "The CEO? The Board? Committees? Opinionated individuals? The whole organization?" They'd been operating for years with ambiguous lines of authority and the exhausting expectation of answering to a host of constituencies.

Their bylaws gave a clear answer: associates work for the CEO. With clarity and confidence, they learned to respect input from all other sources (including board members) but **received the CEO's word as authoritative in daily practice**.

That clarity gave them new peace and fresh air, and stopped the board from the bad habit of doing "end-around" maneuvers that confused everyone.

Here's more:

4. ***Plan periodic check-ups** to see how the model is working.*

5. ***Using the AIP model** (authorization, affirmation, accountability, information, ideas, intervention, prayer, passion, protection), the board chair should ask the CEO, "Is there*

anything you need more or less of?" This gives the CEO a chance to say, "I need more ideas...less intervention...more authorization," or whatever the felt need is. And all of it, of course, can be negotiated with dialogue and mutual understanding.

6. ***Now flip the exercise.*** *Let the CEO ask, "Is there anything on the list—or any other thing— that you need from me?" In my experience,* **most boards ask for more information. At the end of this chapter, you'll find an exercise called "Go AIP" to keep boards informed in useful ways without exhausting executives, and vice versa.** *And the whole organization can practice this exercise by using it to increase information flow.*

7. **Let the board police itself.** *Boards that are shy about putting bullies (usurpers of group process) in their place will put undue pressure on the CEO to defend himself and others. The CEO shouldn't have to manage bad behavior by board members.*

8. *If a potential board member is the type who cannot fathom finding or adding value in a think tank, and perceives himself or herself as "primarily a doer,"* **steer clear of that candidate.** *People who find governing leadership tedious or impractical are proving themselves to be misfits for this level of leadership. They will frustrate and be frustrated. They belong at the operations level of leadership, not the board level.*

9. *Of course,* **boards do need people capable of management.** *Sometimes the board might tackle a new venture or a supplemental operation. Especially in new companies or during transitional seasons, boards need strong managers.*

10. **Involve those who recruit, nominate or select new members--the membership or nominating committee***—in the teaching and implementation of this high-authorization model. The type of people who are enlisted for the board should be people capable of honoring this model—or else they will have a painful and pain-inflicting experience.*

11. *Finally,* **stay with the model for a long season.** *Don't quit before there's some saturation in the culture. Then and only then will it bear the best fruit.*

Whatever the leadership setting, **John Carver** laments that boards can be "**incompetent groups made up of competent people**...mindful people regularly carrying out mindless activity... intelligent people tied up in trivia."[60]

Peter Drucker calls the "decline of the board a **universal phenomenon**" of the last century.[61]

Aubrey Malphurs writes of the "lack of training and understanding" that creates dysfunction, along with the **tendency for power people harbored in boards** to take control and run things.[62]

---

[60] Carver, John. *Boards that Make a Difference: A New Design for Leadership in Non-profit and Public Organizations.* San Francisco: Jossey-Bass, 2006.

[61] Drucker, Peter F. *Management: Tasks, Responsibilities, Practices.* New York: HarperCollins, 1993.

We need models that work and leaders who function together. This model is tried and tested and it can bring fresh wind to your leadership culture.

One more thing—**why not make board work fun**? Tom Sawyer convinced his peers that whitewashing a fence could be a pleasurable adventure. Is it possible that achieving great things together can actually be more enjoyable than most other entertainments we could conjure? I'm not merely suggesting gimmicks and play days, or that every board meeting should meet near the golf course. This is what I am suggesting: **accomplishing worthy goals in a context of community is one of life's greatest joys.**

Even better than whitewashing a fence!

---

[62] Malphurs, Aubrey. *Leading Leaders: Empowering Church Boards for Ministry Excellence.* Grand Rapids: Baker Books, 2005.

Whitewashing the Fence

GO AIP
What do you really need to perform at the highest Possible level? A board, executive and staff worksheet.

Authorization
Do you feel fully authorized for your important work?

Do you feel micromanaged or disrespected as a professional in any way?

Are you performing at a level that warrants the amount of authorization you've been granted?

Affirmation
Do you hear enough verbal affirmation to stay energized and feel appreciated?

Are their other approaches to affirming your contribution that you'd like to see exercised or increased?

Are you performing in ways that warrant a high and authentic level of affirmation?

Accountability

Do you feel that you have too much accountability, too little accountability, or just the right amount?

Do you ever feel abandoned, or as if your supervisor has abdicated real accountability?

Describe the overall health of your programs and projects in relationship to the specific goals that have been set1.

1.

2.

3.

Describe your personal health, family life and energy levels. How are they affecting your work in this season? How is work affecting your health, home and energy?

Information

Do you have enough information about your role and associated hopes and expectations, or is there ambiguity about what you're supposed to be doing day to day? Are lines of authority clear?

Do you know with clarity "the big picture" and where your contributions fit the whole?

Ideas

Are you swimming in ideas, or is the well running dry.

Are your ideas being honored, or do you feel as if others are imposing too much influence on your approach to your task

Would you benefit from visiting other people or places to get ideas or inspiration? If so, where?

Intervention

Are you or your programs/projects at risk in anyway?

Are you placing the wider enterprise at risk in any way?

Prayer

Are you flourishing, growing and expanding as a person?

Are there any crises that affect you day to day?

How is your work environment contributing to your growth and expansion? Do you have concerns or suggestions?

Provision

In order to reach established goals, do you need:
More help?
More resources?
More time?
More _____?

Protection

As you do your work and aspire to reach established goals, do you need:

Someone out ahead to run interference? (Who or what threatens your success?)

Someone to get behind and protect your flank? (Who or what threatens your success?)

Do you feel freedom to innovate and take appropriate risks?

Do you operate out of fear or confidence?

If there are fears, what are you afraid of and how c an we grow your confidence?

Are your contributions to the organization fully defensible and worth protecting?

Other than these AIPs, ...I need_____

Acknowledgements

So many people contributed to this project. First, I think of mentors who taught and encouraged me—Ken Working, Bruce Armstrong, Randy Sundberg, Eldon Pearce, Duane Magee, Daun Brown, Lee Lane, Dave Lipp, Roberta Hestenes, Frank Burr, Don Hadley, Bill Yaeger, Ken Backlund, Maurice Vanderberg, Leron Heath, Stuart Armstrong, Walt Gerber and Kevin Compton. From pastors and policemen to business leaders, teachers, coaches and professors, you've all invested in me. Thank you.

Then I think of many close associates who've proven by your leadership and competence the principles of this book. Since yours is a long list, it seems best to mention only a few in particular. Even in seasons when I was technically "your boss", John Tastad and Phil Vaughn were the most important leaders in my life. Even more, you always saw "the man behind the title" and have followed up with loyal, generous friendship over decades of ups and downs. And I want to mention Sally Bryant and Jackie Hester, two ardent encouragers during the days when I wondered if I could write worthy books.

I'm grateful for the support of Eric and Marguerite McAfee, Bob and Nancy Commins, Keith and Cindy Mueller, Marvin and Kelly Blough, Chris and Hallie Clark, Steve and Lori Stenstrom, Ronnie and Karen Lott, Kim and Kathleen Normington, Sheyna Heard and the late Rev. Jeffrey Heard, Craig and Carrie Elin Awbrey, Carl and Sheri Agers, Carl and Olivia D'Costa, Buck and Ann (Pecota) Sample, Bill and Bobbi Johnson, Bob and Dru Totman, Norman and Muriel Alexander, Harwood Kolsky, and all Friends of Potter's Clay.

The photo on the author's page is by Kirsten Trapani, and her husband Chris has also been so supportive. Jerry Lund did the graphics on the cover and interior. Steve Van Atta provided immeasurable help in editing the manuscript for both content and form and Ron Cassel gave a final once-over with a load of useful commentary and improvements. Ron's wife Karen has been a constant believer in my work.

Finally, I acknowledge that executive leadership is very costly for immediate family. My wife Sue has shared that cost with grace, patience and a genuine belief in my character and competence. She's been a cheerleader, confidante and inspiration.

About the Author

Keith Potter is a passionate, engaging conference speaker and workshop leader. You can host your own *Whitewashing the Fence* Conference or Workshop by contacting Keith at

www.ChampionProject.com or
www.KeithPotter.com or
keith@pottersclayonline.org

Keith bundled up decades of experience in executive leadership and launched into the coaching realm. His great passion is to see high-functioning relationships, clear communication and extraordinary outcomes in every crucial team culture, including the home and workplace.

Unshakable: The Building Blocks of an Enduring Marriage is translated into languages on three continents. Keith teamed with NFL legend Ronnie Lott to produce ***SportsTweet: What I Learned from Coaches About Sports and Life.*** He contributed to ***The Making of a Mentor*** by Ted Engstrom and Ron Jenson and has several other titles in production, including a series of novels—"Stories will forever be the best way to reach and teach."

Keith is a Founding Partner of **Claywork Productions,** Lead Barista for ***The Marriage Café*** movement and the Executive Director of **Potter's Clay**, a non-profit infusion of help and inspiration for marriages, leaders and their organizations.

Keith has Bachelors, Masters and Doctoral degrees from Northwest Christian University and Fuller Theological Seminary, and studied at Western Washington University, the University of Oregon and Bethel Seminary. He lives in Temecula, California, with his wife Sue and their two younger children.

READ <u>other books</u> by Keith Potter

Unshakable
The Building Blocks of an Enduring Marriage

Go to Kindle, Amazon.com or www.MarriageCafeOnline.com

SportsTweet
What I Learned from Coaches About Sports and Life,

by **Ronnie Lott** with **Keith Potter**

(www.ChampionProject.com or Amazon.com

Get ready to READ <u>novels</u> by K. Alan Clay

The Luke Thomas Series

The Body They May Kill
All Mortal Flesh
Even Under the Earth
What Man Tears Asunder
From the Dark Domain

Request a *Whitewashing the Fence Leadership Workshop*

www.ChampionProject.com
www.KeithPotter.com,

Support Keith's non-profit efforts at

www.PottersClayOnline.org

16903837R10117

Made in the USA
Charleston, SC
16 January 2013